THE
PLAYERS'
ADVICE

Seán O'Sullivan is a fan, Gaelic footballer, coach and student in that order. The Dubliner has been involved with his local club, CLG Na Fianna, since he was six years old. He coached his first team when he was only sixteen. Seán is studying for a BSc in Education and Training in DCU. His passion for the GAA drove him to follow his dream to bring this book to life. He is one of the youngest authors ever published by The O'Brien Press. This is his first book.

THE
PLAYERS'
ADVICE

TIPS AND TACTICS FROM GAA STARS

SEÁN O'SULLIVAN

THE O'BRIEN PRESS
DUBLIN

First published 2021 by
The O'Brien Press Ltd,
12 Terenure Road East, Rathgar,
Dublin 6, Ireland
D06 HD27
Tel: +353 1 4923333; Fax: +353 1 4922777
E-mail: books@obrien.ie
Website: www.obrien.ie
The O'Brien Press is a member of Publishing Ireland.

ISBN: 978-1-78849-268-3

Picture credits:
Cover and internal photographs copyright © Sportsfile; used with permission.
Full photography credits:
p 202-203.

Printed and bound by ScandBook AB, Lithuania.
The paper in this book is produced using pulp from managed forests.

Published in:

Self Help Africa

In just over a decade, Galway sports star Alan Kerins has raised several million euro to end the poverty and suffering of tens of thousands of people in rural Southern Africa.

In 2015 Alan teamed up with Self Help Africa, and in partnership is supporting our programmes to end hunger and poverty in Africa.

Alan has been supported by the GAA at both national and grassroots level, and has built up a strong network of supporters across a range of differing sporting codes, including soccer, rugby, boxing and athletics. He has also been backed in his work by figures from the entertainment industry and from across Irish business. His innovative fundraising efforts across Ireland have attracted widespread support and raised millions of euro.

Foreword

By Marty Morrissey

There is nothing worse than a double physics class. Bad enough to have forty minutes of Newton's Laws of Motions or worse still Ohm's Law or a teacher who can't get his head around Archimedes Principle without boring the entire class until you hear snoring coming from the back of the room. Where I went to school, St Flannan's College in Ennis, my physics teacher was Fr Willie Walsh, later to become Bishop Willie. He was in charge of the Harty Cup team, which was the Senior Hurling team in the College, so we always had a plan on the week of the match. Get Fr Willie to talk about the game on Tuesday. We'd play the match on Wednesday and review the match on Thursday, which meant all the physics classes were over for the week! We weren't worried about the Leaving Cert coming down the tracks. Ironically, after graduation I ended up teaching physics, so Fr Willie had a positive impact on my career choice.

But did I ever think about writing a book about my great passion of sport, and GAA in particular, at the back of the physics class? Absolutely not! That's what makes this book and Seán O'Sullivan so fascinating. Having an idea, scribbling down a few thoughts during his physics class just three weeks before his exams in 2019 and then pursuing his idea so that we now have a book that contains advice from over a hundred top-class inter-county players across four codes in twenty-eight counties is a remarkable achievement. Being a former goalkeeper of ill repute, I was intrigued by the advice from Niall Morgan, Gary Connaughton, Enda Rowland, Aoife

Murray, Brendan Cummins, Ciara Trant, Alan O'Mara, Colm Callanan, Brendan Kealy and Eoin Murphy. And they are just the goalkeepers!

I really enjoyed reading this compendium of advice, wisdom and lessons learned on the field of play from GAA players from every code. Seeing these players share tips and experiences with young and up and coming players epitomises the community spirit of the GAA where traditions and knowledge are passed down within clubs and communities. For a young man in his Leaving Cert year to have both the idea for this book and the initiative and persistence to bring it to fruition is very impressive. Seán O'Sullivan has created a great resource; the variety of advice and topics covered by players from every code, who play in every position across the pitch, means that anyone with an interest in GAA is sure to find something for them.

I hope Gaelic players, coaches and fans alike enjoy and learn from this useful book.

Yours in sport,

Marty Morrissey

Marty Morrissey is an Irish sports commentator and television presenter. He regularly presents high-profile sports events for RTÉ Sport, such as the All-Ireland Senior Football Championship and Olympic Games.

Foreword

By Mick Bohan

What a fantastic achievement for a young man to have pulled a piece of work together like this.

What a positive reflection on the GAA community nationwide for so many young people to have taken time out to share some of the nuggets that they have picked up during the course of their careers with a young man the majority of them hadn't met before.

Our games are special and they grip us from an early age, they give us an identity, a pastime, a place of refuge, an escape and a purpose. They give us friendships, they teach us how to deal with upset and failure, and sometimes when we are really fortunate we experience the absolute satisfaction of victory.

This book shares the many stories, lessons and nuggets that players have learnt or had passed on to them down through the years.

Here are some of the things I've learned over the years.

When I started coaching I thought I couldn't find enough drills; I was always watching other teams train, purchasing different sports manuals or seeking out any book that I possibly could that would have some diagram of some pattern of movement that I could imitate.

I never really asked why, I just wanted the movement to look well, without really understanding what the purpose of it was. As the years went on, I realised whatever patterns of movement you practise, your players will play, so I moved on to game-relative patterns of movement, the real stuff, what takes place in the game.

There in front of your eyes is your playbook: watch the game, see how you open up space or close it down, how you shift the ball to places on the field where there is space and create openings that looked locked down a few seconds earlier. This is where your real playbook is formed.

The other thing that changed was listening to the players, getting their feedback on what worked and what didn't, what made sense and what confused them; the learnings they themselves took from the 'arena'.

Simple things like where their feet should be when run at, the positional space a fellow forward needed to create in order to give time for their teammate to get a strike off. The things that gave their biggest disappointments, like not realising their potential; that's probably the biggest fear and so it should be!

The key learnings in the language they use like 'don't make the first move' when a forward is running at you or 'the power of doing nothing' when a forward holds out rather than getting lost in the crowd as their team attack.

Our job is to pass on the nuggets and there are so many of them in this book.

Enjoy, learn from it and share the gems from the players who played in the arena.

My favourite phrase in coaching is 'the key moments of the game are decided by executing the simple things really well'.

Enjoy the read. I certainly did.

Ádh mór

Mick Bohan

Mick Bohan is the current Dublin Ladies football manager. He has worked as a coach with multiple Dublin teams including Development Squads, Minors, u21s, Men, Ladies and with the Clare Footballers. Between underage, colleges, men's and ladies' football, he has played a part in winning fifteen national titles.
One of the leading coaches in the country, he has transformed the Jackies into a powerful force, winning four All-Irelands in a row.

Contents

Introduction

I had the idea to put this book together during a double physics class about three weeks before my Leaving Cert back in 2019. I started scribbling down names of players I felt I could get to contribute at the time; I had no idea it would grow into this. Over the past eighteen months I have been contacting the top footballers, hurlers and camogie players from all over the country, asking for any advice they have for players. With twenty-eight counties represented and 107 players participating, as far as I know this book is the first of its kind.

Within this book you will find advice on a range of areas that affect your game on and off the pitch. Topics such as gym, nutrition, routine, lifestyle, skills, mindset and preparation. The questions and topics raised throughout the book are a mix of my own and questions from a survey of over three hundred players in my own club, CLG Na Fianna.

In terms of the player recruitment for this book, I went for players I look up to, players I admire and players I thought would have something interesting or worthwhile to say. Also, they are all from my lifetime, so the past twenty years. I probably reached out to between two and three hundred players across all thirty-two counties.

All players have taken different paths and journeys to get where they are, using different approaches and methods in developing their game. There are still some overlaps, which shows what might have worked for a majority of these players. There are also some contradictions; some players believe it's beneficial to try your hand at multiple sports when you're young, others think your best chance is to dedicate yourself to one sport and thrive at it. At the end of the day these are their opinions, formed from years of playing and training at the highest level. As well as what readers can learn from the players, they advise turning to coaches or trusted professionals when it comes to specific nutrition, strength and conditioning (S&C) or injury advice.

This is a mix of interviews, voice messages and pieces written by the players themselves. The pieces of advice written by the players have taken different styles due to their individual style of writing. Some have used specific headings, some have written theirs more like essays and some have been ghost-written by me. The book has been laid out like a team starting with Goalkeepers, Full Backs, Half Backs, etc. I've put the players into what I believe is their best position.

Obviously, you will learn more from reading each piece of advice instead of those just in your position. It's very possible if you play in the forwards you will pick up something from the backs and vice-versa.

The purpose of this book is to help you get from where you are, to where you want to be. Whether it's out onto the pitch in Croke Park or into your team's starting fifteen, the priceless advice throughout will surely give you a chance to reach your full potential.

'If there's a book that you want to read, but it hasn't been written yet, then you must write it.' I like to think that's what I've done here. I hope you enjoy.

Seán O'Sullivan
2021

Gary Connaughton

Aoife Murray

Eoin Murphy

Brendan Cummins

THE GOALKEEPERS' ADVICE

Niall Morgan

Ciara Trant

Brendan Kealy
KERRY FOOTBALLER 2010-2017

Kealy made his senior debut during the 2010 National League; he immediately became a regular member of the starting fifteen, winning seven Munster Championships during his career. He won an All-Ireland in 2014, followed by an All-Star in 2015. He is currently Kerry's goalkeeping coach and also runs a page on social media 'thegaagk' where he posts tips and drills for goalkeepers to develop and improve.

Advice for a young Goalkeeper

One of the most common questions I get asked by young 'keepers is 'How can I make my kickout better/longer?' My answer is always the same – focus on technique rather than length. If you can get your kicking technique right, then the rest will follow and as you get older the length and power of your kick will naturally increase.

In terms of perfecting your technique, begin by kicking off the grass in an unstructured type of way. For example, just kicking around with a friend, 'soccer style', and not placing the ball deliberately before each kick. This helps to train the body and brain to work out different ways of manipulating the ball for different types of kicks (i.e. hooking, curling, slicing, drilling, chipping etc.) as it is not always going to be lying perfectly on the grass. Being able to kick the ball cleanly off the grass is very important as it allows for a wider variety of kicks, including free-kicks and 45s, and if you do choose to use a tee you are then more likely to use a lower tee. I feel I have greater control over the ball when I kick off the grass or use a low tee. Another positive thing about this approach is that you don't always need somebody with you to practise it and you don't have to be running around the field chasing footballs. Kicking into a net is ideal for improving technique, such as the large net behind the goals or else into the goal itself. Why? Well, if we are kicking to a target out the pitch we naturally tend to focus on reaching that target, whereabouts on the field has the ball landed – 45-yard line, halfway line ... By removing this it allows us to focus on things like hitting the sweet spot on the ball, keeping your head up to see what's on, what type of run-up suits best (ideally a two or three step run so it is difficult for opposition to read your kick and you can get it out there quicker) and a punchy, driven type of strike. Over time you will know by the connection when you strike the ball if it is an acceptable kick or not. Then progress it onto the pitch where you introduce a target out the field. They can be stationary or moving, or even boxes marked out with cones.

As with any skill, repetition is key and it's the work you do outside of the days you train with your team that will make the difference. Getting over to the pitch on your own to work on things like this kicking practice, arriving early before training to go through this routine so that once training begins you are already a step ahead, making sure that in between sessions you are stretching and improving your mobility (particularly hips and shoulders for goalkeepers), getting adequate sleep and nutrition ... all of this helps massively and makes it all more enjoyable. And at the end of the day that's what it's all about, enjoyment! If you are enjoying yourself on the pitch then that will shine through in how you play.

Eoin Murphy
KILKENNY HURLER 2011-PRESENT

The complete goalkeeper, since breaking into the Kilkenny team Murphy has proven to be one of the top goalkeepers in the country. The two-time All-Star captained WIT to a Fitzgibbon title in 2014, lining out at centre-back. A key part of the Cats' recent success, he has won four National Leagues, six Leinster titles and four All-Irelands. He has also won a Kilkenny Junior Championship, Leinster Championship and All-Ireland Championship with his club, Glenmore.

Skill:

Skill is the easiest attribute to practise, but probably ignored the most. When I was younger, I wasn't blessed with speed or physical size so had to rely solely on being very, very skilful. I practised my striking off both sides every day and with that comes a good first touch. The basics of hurling, such as first touch, catching, striking off both sides need to be developed from an early age. The gym work can come as you're older and in your late teens.

Nutrition:

Something that has become vital in more recent years is teams' prep for matches and even training. Once gym work becomes compulsory and training gets harder on the body, the players have to fuel their bodies in the right way. Everyone is completely different so no black and white template can be used, but depending on the type of training the body will need protein and carbohydrates. It's also very important to be taking on enough water each day. Going to training or matches dehydrated will lead to poor performance and eventually injury.

Shane Curran
ROSCOMMON FOOTBALLER 1990-2005

One of the only players to play in Croke Park across four different decades, 'Cake' was a goalkeeper ahead of his time with his rampaging runs beyond his own 45, free taking and even penalty taking. His honours include a Connacht minor medal in 1989, a Connacht title in 2001, an All-Star nomination in 2003, six Roscommon club titles, two Connacht club titles and an All-Ireland club title 2013 with St Brigid's.

Football, sport and indeed life has changed so much since I started out. There are many outside influences that help us make informed or uninformed decisions regarding our sporting and life ambitions.

When I started you were criticised by your manager or maybe some teammates. This criticism was for your own good, helping to make you a better player and in some cases a better person. Nowadays there are 'keyboard warriors' in every room, every crevice they can find to spout some form of abuse to anyone who dares become much better than they in their chosen sport or career.

For me this is one of the biggest challenges facing young guys and girls. How you deal with setbacks, defeats and uninformed critics will have a major impact on your mental health and your ability to perform to your maximum in your chosen discipline. Some will take it personally, others will continue through the barriers and come out better players/athletes over the course of their careers.

There are many choices young people have to make when deciding to commit large chunks of your time to an amateur game. These may have consequences, loss of career opportunities, loss of social time, and in some cases financial loss due to committing time and energy to sport.

On the flip side, sport offers up huge opportunities. Lifelong friendships are forged. The discipline of practice, good routines – maybe not so good routines after celebrations or disappointments – are all important things to experience. To be successful or indeed to maximise your abilities; practice is a vital pillar of gaining improvement. Gary Player, the world-renowned golfer, once said, 'the more I practised the luckier I got.' I appreciated that quote more as I got older.

There's also the notion that one can't enjoy the normal things in life. Of course, one must be disciplined but it's important to enjoy some fun, a few sociable drinks, eat the odd greasy chip or Chinese, have your holiday, enjoy family or friends' days out. If you're not allowing yourself these excursions, you're highly unlikely to enjoy the huge commitment it takes to become the best you can be.

You hear a lot of comments about sacrifice and you do sacrifice certain things, however no matter what you choose to do there's sacrifice. My advice garnered from twenty-five years playing inter-county and senior club football along with almost ten years as a League of Ireland soccer player, is enjoy, keep everything in perspective and above all keep good company and friends.

Yours in sport,
Shane Curran.

Brendan Cummins
TIPPERARY HURLER 1995-2013

Following his retirement, Cummins has been remembered as one of the greatest of all time. At underage he won a Munster Minor championship, followed by an u21 Munster and All-Ireland Championships. His shot-stopping ability and booming puckouts (he's won the Poc Fada nine times) made him a pivotal figure for the Premier County. The five-time All-Star won four National Leagues, five Munster championships and two All-Irelands during his long career. Cummins first represented the county's footballers and was then a dual player until 2002. With his club Ballybacon-Grange, the Sunday Game pundit has won eleven South Tipperary IHC and a Tipperary JHC.

How do you puck the ball so far?

When I was younger, I had a small enough back garden, about 25 yards long by 15 yards wide. I used to play a game where it was my left side against my right. I'd use one of the cheap plastic footballs, when the air goes from them and if there's frost on them, they get wicked heavy. I'd puck that up and down the garden for all the world. Later, my father put up a mini goal and I tried to hit the crossbar, again it was my left side vs my right side. I think that definitely helped when I was younger.

As I got older, I'd use sliotars, but I used to put them in water overnight to make them heavier. When I'd hit them, they wouldn't go far but when I got a new ball it'd travel miles. I felt there was no need for press-ups or anything like that, it was about the timing, and strengthening your wrists was the key for me.

What's the biggest change that you had to make to your own game?

The puckouts. I was always good at shot-stopping, but hitting out the ball was an issue. Eamonn O'Shea took over with Liam Sheedy in 2008. I changed my swing in how I hit the ball and it became more accurate. They developed a relationship between the forwards and myself, we had a handful of set puckouts, but the idea was that they knew what I was trying to do and I knew what they were trying to do. Through this the relationship became stronger and better. With my practice and more communication between the giver and the receiver, I got better at that and suddenly we began to play better as a team.

That was probably the biggest challenge I had. I'd like to think I overcame it in 2008/2009, that's when I really got it right – changing the way I hit the ball and getting that understanding between me and the forwards.

How do you keep your head up when you make a mistake?

I think it comes through practice, and an understanding that it's not a game of perfect you're playing, it's a game of hurling. Normally if I let in a goal, I'd get thick and then I'd forget about the mistake because I'm so busy trying to make sure it doesn't happen again, and my concentration levels go up. I believe 99 percent of the time when you make an error, it's just a lack of concentration. That can happen because we're all human beings and we're all a bit flawed.

I used to use triggers. You don't get up every day and feel like you're going to take on the world, but if you're playing a championship match and you've had a fight with the girlfriend, failed an exam the day before or maybe had a row at work, you have to have something that runs the happy tape in your head. I used triggers to keep myself in the moment and not think about a minute ago, just think about the next second. There is a technique to that and I was lucky to work with Declan Kyle, my sports psychologist. I was able to develop a technique that was so strong that the whole place could've fallen down around me and I still would have just worried about the next ball.

I had a couple of things to use as triggers. One was I'd double blink. If I was in training in Dr Morris Park and I pulled off a good save, I'd blink twice really quickly to hold the memory. Another trigger was airplanes, the jet stream coming out the back of an airplane. Sometimes trying to explain these things, they sound completely irrational but at the time perfectly natural. When we played in Páirc Uí Chaoimh or Croke Park, you can see the planes taking off from the goals at the Davin end over the back of Hill 16 from the airport. The way I'd think of it was, 'Jesus, there's more going on in the world than what's happening in here, so why should I be so worried about it?' Also, it reminded me of training, when planes would fly over Dr Morris Park into Shannon airport, so it kind of took me back there and made me more comfortable. That comfort is what you want. You don't want to be in Croke Park thinking, 'there's 80,000 people here, that's 160,000 pairs of eyes plus probably a million people watching around the world.' You don't want to go down that road in your head because you'd go out of your mind.

You need something that grounds you. That's what worked for me. Some players write stuff on their arms, others write it on the hurley, other lads might listen to music. I used the same four songs all the time from 2006 on, going into matches. I played well in a league game in 2006 and it was the first time I used music. I swapped some songs in and out but I kept four of them all the time. One of them was Charlotte Church 'It's the heart that matters most', I used it because of the lyrics.

'Time to spread some hope,

Make the spirits rise

Do you see the wonder in their eyes?'

They mean a lot. When I used to look out the side of the bus, going into a championship match, I used to always focus on the kids. That took a lot of the pressure away from me, because they were coming to watch Tipperary win. I was going to be a part of that and all I wanted to do was make them happy. When you're not thinking about yourself, more often than not you're not nervous. If you think about most of the time in life when you get nervous, you're really thinking about the consequences on you and that's why you're nervous. If you think that you're going to look after somebody or you're going to do something for someone else, then you'll find that you're always less nervous doing it.

What's the best piece of advice you were given during your career?

It was from Eamonn O'Shea. I was dropped in 2007. Before the 2008 Munster final, Eamonn came over to me as we were warming up in UL. I asked Eamonn, 'What do you want me to do today?' He looked me straight in the eye and said, 'Just be yourself.' That was the best advice because I didn't know going into a Munster final, having been dropped the year before, should I do something different or what had I to prove. 'Just be yourself'. That was hands-down the best advice I ever got.

What's the most important part of being a goalkeeper? How would you practise it?

Composure. You develop it through exposure. You practise it by training as often as you can, at as high an intensity as you can.

Keep it simple

No matter what way the game changes, the mental part of the game stays the same. Skill is a given. It's how you cope with the pressure that allows you to express yourself. That's what separates the great players from the good ones. That's from my experience of hurling.

Gary Connaughton
WESTMEATH FOOTBALLER 2003-2015

Since hanging up his boots, Connaughton has been remembered as one of Westmeath's greatest players. Following his retirement in 2013, he returned to the Westmeath seniors as a player/selector. He is one of the county's most successful players with an All-Star, a Leinster title and two National Leagues.

My advice to younger people who play sport is always to enjoy it and learn from an early age the basic skills of their chosen sport. My chosen sport was football and the game is always about what you can do with the ball. Every young kid should always have a ball and be constantly practising with both feet from an early age. This will stand to them when they get older and are involved with their club team and if they are lucky, with their county team. Strength and conditioning are seen by many nowadays as important but for anyone between the ages of twelve and eighteen, practising the basic skills like kicking, catching, fielding and shooting are what will improve them to be a good footballer.

I played in goal in both GAA and soccer at different stages of my younger years. I was always seeking ways of improving my game, so I was constantly kicking a ball on a daily basis, either in the field at the back of my house, training sessions with my club or a kick about in the schoolyard.

Kick outs are seen as a vital part of today's game. I would have done a huge amount of cycling at a young age and that stood to me as I got older as it strengthened my legs and that enabled me to get extra distance in the kick out. Also, I would place cones around the pitch in training sessions and practise hitting the ball towards the cones for accuracy and this improved my distribution as I progressed to the County senior team.

When I was seventeen, I had a trial at Newcastle United soccer club in England whereby I was training on a daily basis with professional goalkeepers such as former Ireland international, Shay Given. I learned as much as I could from this training and when I returned home, I incorporated a lot of the drills into my training routine.

Nowadays, all GAA goalkeepers normally train together and this is what young goalkeepers should look to do as they don't need to be training with outfield players. Handling, speed and agility drills, feet work and shot-stopping are the main aspects of a goalkeeping training session. There are plenty of videos on YouTube in regards to this type of training, especially for younger goalkeepers.

I would recommend for any aspiring young keeper that they should be studying Stephen Cluxton and how he performs on the day of a match. The way he positions himself in the goal, how he deals with shot-stopping and the high ball and also his leadership qualities on the field of play. You can see how cool, calm and collected he is in the goal and how focused he stays throughout the whole seventy minutes of a game.

First and foremost, if you're a young player, concentrate on your education. Your education is your main priority; you can always find a balance around playing sport and studying. Always enjoy your sport and learn as much as you can from your managers and coaches. Listen and respect the advice you get from them. Work hard at your game and always believe in yourself that you can play at a high level.

Aoife Murray
CORK CAMOGIE PLAYER 2002-2020

Since walking away from inter-county, Murray has been remembered as one of the all-time greats. The former Rebelettes captain brought a professional approach to the art of goalkeeping, winning eight All-Stars. The 2008 POTY won five National Leagues and nine All-Irelands during her time with the Leesiders. She has also won three Cork championships with her club, Cloughduv.

Advice to my younger self:

Teenage years for me were a maze, it was a strange place between being a child and an adult. Looking back now I think I would tell my teenage self not to be so hard on my body and mind; I am paying for it physically and emotionally now. I would go from playing volleyball where I would be diving on wood flooring to diving on a worn-out piece of goalmouth. I think of the advice physios gave me that I didn't take, playing was more important to me. If I missed a match, would that be the game a Cork selector was watching and had I missed the opportunity of showing my potential?

Every second I could spend on the pitch meant more than any possible physical hurt or long-term damage. I was a camogie player first and a growing, maturing young woman second. And a failing on my part is if I was back there, I would probably do the same all over again. Playing is like a drug, it can completely blind you like a horse with blinkers on. It was more important than making friends, winning was the finishing line.

So to that end I would advise you to talk to someone outside of your bubble, someone that sees you not as the hurler/player, someone who doesn't know what it is like to be obsessed with the sport – it might help to stop beating yourself up mentally and emotionally. If you are good enough you will be seen. Remember, smile, you're doing something you love.

Niall Morgan
TYRONE FOOTBALLER 2013-PRESENT

Morgan broke into the Tyrone senior team in 2013, he has since proved to be one of the top goalkeepers in the country, winning two Ulster titles in 2016 and 2017 and earning an All-Star nomination in 2017. Morgan has also represented Ireland in three International Rules Series in 2014, 2015 and 2017.

Skill Development:

The most important thing is to test yourself in the basic skills. If you are right footed, practise pick-ups, solos and kicks with your left. Catching the ball first time is so important because if you have a poor first touch, it doesn't matter how good you are on the ball as you might not get a second chance to have it in your hands. Forget about the fancy stuff and work on catching, fist passing and kicking as often as you possibly can – all you need is a ball and a wall!

Mindset:

You are only as good as your BEST game – if you have played that well before then you can do it again. Don't get too high with the highs of football and likewise don't get too low with the lows. You may lose a big game at some point in your career, but playing on a team is about more than just a medal – the joy and pride you get out of representing others, be it club, county, province or country is more than anything a medal can give you.

Advice for your younger self:

Enjoy the process more. I always got caught up in winning, but feel I could have been better at bringing others along with me and in turn creating more of a winning environment. Being a leader is about more than having the skills to play the game – it's about helping others to want to achieve and learn as much as you do.

Enda Rowland
LAOIS HURLER 2015-PRESENT

An integral part of Laois's recent rise to the top table, Rowland has established himself among the top keepers in today's game. The 2019 All-Star nominee has proven to be one of the best long-range free takers in the country. The Laois captain lead his team to a Joe McDonagh Cup victory in 2019 and has also represented Ireland in two International Rules Series.

Gym and Nutrition

Probably the area of the game that has seen the most change in the last number of years. As a goalkeeper, I'd be big into the gym for rotational and core strength. It's important to work the same muscles I'd be using for puck-outs and when a forward is coming in it's important to be able to come out and stand your ground. For outfield players you have got to be able to take the hits and bounce back up again. The important thing for young players is to get your technique right, correct squat, plank, push up etc. There's no point doing the gym work if you don't eat right, because they'll just cancel each other out. Both have to go hand in hand, correctly. Definite advice for any young players coming up would be eat healthy and eat all the right foods, all natural, nothing processed, that's very important.

Preparation and Skill Development

For me, I'd always be thinking and preparing for games. Thinking about what you're going to do and what you've done in previous matches. Having my gear ready and arriving on time. For both hurling and football, you're expected to have a good touch, expected to be able to use both sides. It's part and parcel of the game now. Like gym and nutrition, you have to do these things in your own time. Working on your touch, working on your striking. Players nowadays are so talented and so skilful that that's the level you have to get to.

Advice for my younger self

When I was younger, diet would have been a major issue for me. I'd always be out practising; I'd always do the other things right. The one thing that let me down would've been my diet. It took me a while to change, it took a setback or two for me to realise I had to change my diet. My advice to my younger self as a thirteen or fourteen-year-old would be start trying new foods and try all the healthy foods, because they are nice. If I had exposed myself to more knowledge about nutrition at a younger age it would've helped massively since it wasn't until I was about twenty that I started taking it seriously.

Ciara Trant
DUBLIN FOOTBALLER 2015-PRESENT

With a blistering u21 career, winning back-to-back All Irelands in 2014 and 2015, it was almost inevitable that Trant would join the senior ranks. Making her debut in the National Football league against Monaghan, she has played in the All-Ireland final every year since. Winning two National Leagues, four All-Irelands and two All-Stars, she has proven to be one of the top goalkeepers in the country.

It's easy to get swallowed up by nutrition, gym work, tactics, and the latest fads. It's essential to remember why you're there, how you got there and ultimately what you want to achieve. It's easy to lose touch with yourself. I constantly remind myself that I am living my dream. Growing up, through my teenage years, and even when I was twenty and on the fringe of the panel, I dreamed of pulling on the jersey and lining out for Dublin. Every time I put on the Dublin crest, for training or a match, I remind myself that doing just that was and still is the dream. Realising that and not taking it for granted has made me work harder. The knock-on has been success. So my advice is to ground yourself in the bigger picture, your bigger picture. As kids we play and we dream. As adults, in order to reach our potential, we must play and we must dream.

Alan O'Mara
CAVAN FOOTBALLER 2013-2017

Alan O'Mara is the founder of Real Talks and a renowned speaker on the topics of health and wellbeing. He hosts the Real Talks podcast series. As an Ulster u21 champion with Cavan, he became the first active senior inter-county player to go public about experiencing depression in 2013. He is currently completing a Masters in Sports and Exercise Psychology and is a wellbeing ambassador to the HSE's 'Little Things' campaign. To learn more about Alan or his work, go to www.RealTalks.ie

I once went from playing in an All-Ireland u21 Final in Croke Park to being consumed by suicidal thoughts and feelings within six months. Reaching out for help in my darkest hour is the most important thing I have ever accomplished.

Counselling taught me that happiness was an inside job and that I should never be solely reliant on winning a game of football or playing well to feel good about myself. Sport is a huge part of my life and always will be, but it no longer defines me. Learning to be open and honest about my thoughts, feelings and emotions has strengthened my relationships with the people I care about rather than make them more difficult. Managing my mind-set and lifestyle has made me a better, more resilient person.

Life challenges us all in many different ways as we get older – exams, sport, bullies, family, relationships and financial pressures to name just a few. You will have good days and bad days and that is okay.

If a bad day ever becomes a bad week or a bad week becomes a bad month, know that help can come in many different forms. If you ever feel like I did, you don't have to tell everyone. Just tell one person. Open up to a parent, a friend, a boyfriend, a girlfriend, a brother, a sister, a teacher or a coach. Depression tries to make you feel like you are the only person in the world to feel that way but it is simply not the case. That is why wonderful organisations like Pieta House, Samaritans and SpunOut.ie exist.

Mind yourself, look out for others and help build more compassionate communities throughout Ireland.

Colm Callanan
GALWAY HURLER 2007-2019

A key part of Galway's 2017 All-Ireland success, Callanan proved to be a top-class shot-stopper over his thirteen-year career, winning two National Leagues and two Leinster titles. He has also won a Galway Intermediate Championship with his club, Kinvara. Following his retirement, the 2015 All-Star is now a selector in the Tribesmen's backroom team.

THERE ARE SEVEN THINGS FIT PEOPLE DO EVERY DAY.

They Stick to Their Plan

Who wouldn't love to come home from a long day of school or work and watch a marathon of their favourite TV show? The fit make exercise a priority and stick to their guns. Try this: when you get home from school change immediately into your workout gear.

Avoid sitting on the couch or lying down and begin your workout immediately. Whether you're streaming your workout or plan to hit the road again on your way to the gym just keep moving before your mind has an opportunity to talk you out of it.

Another option is to work out first thing in the morning before your body knows what's going on!

They Sleep

Sleep can re-energize and reinvigorate you. That's no surprise, but research shows that cutting back on sleep causes increased feelings of hunger, less satisfaction after meals, and a lack of energy to exercise, thus causing a reduction of fat loss in comparison to well rested individuals.

They Mix Up Their Routine

Mixing up your routine nixes the boredom that comes with moving on an elliptical machine for thirty minutes every day. Do yoga one day, interval training the next, and strength training the following day. If your fitness routine doesn't bore you, you're more likely to stick to it.

They Focus on the Feeling

Working out isn't always fun while you're doing it, but the endorphin high you get after – or the myriad other benefits, like a sound night of sleep and positive body image are.

They Eat Real Food

The fit aim to eat food that is as close to nature as possible and drastically limit processed foods. It's a process that doesn't just happen overnight. Don't swear off certain food groups. You'll be miserable, binge, feel bad, and then swear off all that food AGAIN and the cycle will repeat, and you'll feel worse every time! Increase your lean protein intake and work to integrate more fruits and vegetables into every meal a little more every day.

They Exercise Even If It Is Only for Fifteen Minutes

A short routine is better than nothing and fit people know this. You don't need to spend an hour on a workout to reap the benefits of exercise.

They Move Every Day

The fit are not afraid to move! They park farther away, skip the elevator, and when sitting at a desk for eight hours a day, they get up to move every thirty to forty-five minutes. If you can't possibly bear to get to the gym after work, just five or ten minutes of exercise can help you get moving.

Keith Higgins

Eoghan O'Donnell

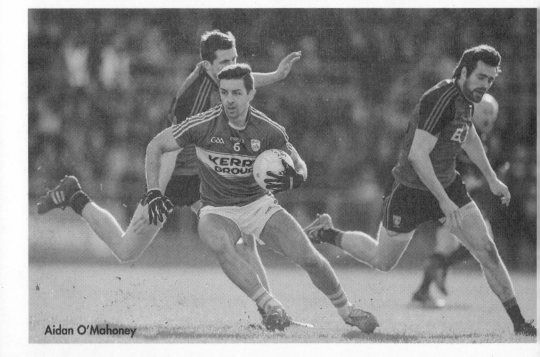

Aidan O'Mahoney

Cathal Barrett

THE FULLBACKS' ADVICE

Pamela Mackey

Brid Stack

Jonny Cooper
DUBLIN FOOTBALLER 2012-PRESENT

Dublin's go-to defender has always played his best football on the edge. A key part of Dublin's five-in-a-row winning team his reading of the game is second to none. The Na Fianna man has enjoyed a raft of success in his career; All-Ireland u21 winning captain 2010, two Sigersons as DCU captain, five National Leagues, eight Leinster titles, seven All-Irelands and two All-Stars.

First thing that is important is to respect your parent(s)/guardians and teachers by saying 'thank you' as often as you can and making them feel appreciated. The next important element is to ensure that your club provides you and your friends with a supportive and challenging environment where you can go for things in a safe environment, knowing not everything will work the way you want it to.

When everything above is in place, you can start to work on key traits such as discipline, hard work and honesty. Very often the top players have had to go through many failures so you need to realise that success (whatever that is) is not a straight line. Discipline looks like being on time, eating the right foods, drinking water and going to the gym. Hard work is doing extra schoolwork, asking your teachers questions on how to understand something, and doing study when your friends are out playing. Honesty is practising often again and again and again, it is telling a teammate or friend how you are feeling and it is doing an extra five runs knowing that you always have 20 percent more in you.

There is no set script you need to follow. Doctors, musicians, astronauts, teachers and GAA players are not born that way. They each work hard, respect what they have and have the discipline to shape whatever future they want to have.

Cathal Barrett

TIPPERARY HURLER 2014-PRESENT

Barrett had a memorable debut season in 2014, reaching the All-Ireland final against Kilkenny. Although he was on the losing side following a replay, he was named Young Hurler of the Year for that season. Since then he has won two Munster titles in 2015 and 2016, an All-Star in 2016 and two All-Ireland medals in 2016 and 2019.

Young players these days need to be more committed than ever before. Even at club level commitment has gone through the roof. The days of training once or twice a week have gone and you have to be willing to go the extra mile to succeed in your sport. You train with your team two or three times a week and you do your own bit after, be it in the gym, recovery, wall ball, yoga etc. It's about keeping up with the progression and not being left behind.

Set out your goals early and strive for them every day. Look for that extra 1 per cent, whether it's your diet, skill, preparation, whatever it is you're always looking to gain something. Being willing to make sacrifices is massive. You can't stay out until all hours with your friends when you have training the next morning. If you do you're not giving yourself the best chance to improve and make those hard gains needed to reach the standards you've set yourself.

The most important skill in hurling is attitude. You could have wrists like Bubbles O'Dwyer or the strength of Paudie Maher, but if you're not turning up with the right attitude and the overalls on to go and work, then all the skill in the world can't help you. Having that desire to win every dirty ball and beat your man no matter what, will define you as a player and all that starts in the training field. You have to go through the hard slog of training in the muck and building that hard resilience in order to bring out the work you've banked on the big days. It's not like switching on a lightbulb, you cannot just turn it on. It has to be prepared and fed days, weeks, months before the games. Building it from the ground up. Respect every teammate and coach and try to learn something from everyone you meet. Your life outside of sport falls into this category. You can't expect hurling to get you good grades and good jobs, you have to work hard and earn them. Hurling is great and is one of the best things you will ever do in life, but if you don't secure a future for yourself for after sport then no matter what you have accomplished on the field I would deem it a failure. Balance is key. You apply the same drive and attitude to your studies and jobs as you do to your training. It will make the road much easier and open many doors in your life. They will complement each other, and you'll be a happier person for it.

If I was to give advice to my younger self it would be to go to players that had done it before me, ask them what mistakes they made on their way and make sure I don't make the same. Give myself every chance to achieve what I want to achieve in both sport and in my personal life with studies and work. Enjoy every minute of your sporting days because it's so precious and doesn't last forever.

Shane Enright
KERRY FOOTBALLER 2011-2021

Making his senior debut in 2011, Enright was entrusted as Kerry's man marker, generally picking up the opposition's 'danger-man'. Enright enjoyed great success with the Kingdom, winning eight Munster titles, an All-Ireland in 2014 and an All-Star in 2016.

Nutrition

When I was younger I didn't take as much care with my nutrition as I do now. When I started off playing with Kerry, we might have had a nutritionist in once a year to have a chat with us to help make sure we ate the correct foods. Nowadays we have a full-time nutritionist which is a great help. Making sure that you are eating the correct foods at specific times of the year/week based on your training load is key. It is very important when we are doing heavy training sessions to ensure that the body is loaded up with carbohydrates to provide energy for the training session ahead. Similarly it is essential that plenty of protein is taken on board after training to ensure that the body recovers as quickly as possible in order to be ready for the next training session. Hydration is key at all times throughout the season. Water is essentially like oil for the car, it ensures that the body is in good order and you aren't cramping up during training sessions. Nowadays players take a lot of supplements to help out with nutrition also such as pre fuel energy drinks and gels that provide the body with instant sources of energy pre match or training sessions (always take advice from your coach or a nutritionist before starting on any supplements). Snacking is also a big part of an inter-county footballer's diet. Fruit and nuts are frequently taken in between meals to ensure that the body is getting all the nutrients required to perform at the highest level.

Gym

Gaelic footballers have become strong, athletic, powerful footballers from the increased work done in the gym which has taken the game to a whole new level over the last number of years. Gym programmes are now tailored for each player based on the different aspects of his physique that need to be worked on. Gym work is done pretty much all year round now to ensure that the body is kept in good nick and muscle isn't lost in the off season. Most inter-county teams get back to the gym doing collective sessions in November to ensure that plenty of work will be done before the start of the new season.

Gym work is essential in the prevention of injuries as well as allowing players to build muscle and condition the body for the long inter-county season ahead. Players try and get to the gym maybe three times a week in the off season when there aren't too many games being played. This allows players to lift heavier weights in order to allow for muscle growth during a time when they don't have to worry about performing in big games. When the inter-county season is back in full flow, two gym sessions a week is adequate, with one being a strength session at the start of the week and the second being more of a power session where less weight is lifted, allowing the body to be fresh for the important game coming up that weekend.

Domhnall O'Donovan
CLARE HURLER 2010-2016

With his club Clonlara, O'Donovan has won Clare and Munster Intermediate Championships in 2007 only to add a senior Clare title the following year. Off the back of Munster and All-Ireland u21 successes, he added a Fitzgibbon with NUIG to his trophy cabinet. His performances in these competitions alerted the senior setup of his potential. A crucial part of Clare's All-Ireland success in 2013, his only point in championship came in the 72nd minute of the drawn match to force the replay that Clare then won.

If I was to advise my younger self of anything, two things come to mind and I believe they transcend sport into many areas of life.

Don't worry about what you can't control

I worried too much when I was younger and it only led to unnecessary stress. Most often, whatever I worried about or speculated over never actually happened or wasn't that severe. The best thing to do is to focus on you and what you can control in your environment. This comes down to being a bit more calculated in diagnosis of an issue. If you want to make an inter-county team, there is no point sweating over the possibility that Davy Fitz might be at your club championship game. There is however value in the time you devote to preparation for that game – and preparation is not necessarily the night before a game, or the few days before it, but rather a commitment to lifestyle.

Don't hide from a challenge

Firstly, I think it is important to be passionate about something. If you have a passion for something, normally you will be willing to work on it and commit to it. Sometimes this involves leaving one's comfort zone. I remember when I went to trials for the Clare Minor Panel (age sixteen, turning seventeen), I was told the reason I did not make the panel was that I was too small even though I thought my trial had gone quite well. That hurt a lot and I could not believe that a physical limitation (effectively my height and weight) was going to prevent me from achieving my ambitions of playing for Clare. I went to the weight room, I went running, cycling, sprinting – all throughout that year. It was not fun for a lot of it, but I embraced it. The point is that I had spent years just doing the parts of training I loved, but it's important to focus on the parts that you don't enjoy. They will improve you as an all-round athlete as well as strengthen your mind for future challenges.

Ger Cafferkey
MAYO FOOTBALLER 2009-2019

Cafferkey enjoyed a successful u21 career, winning three Connacht titles between 2006 and 2008 and an All-Ireland u21 in 2006. As a senior player the 2012 All-Star added to his success, winning six Connacht titles in a row and a National League title in 2019.

Being very honest, I was a very average footballer. However, I won an All-Star in 2012 probably through hard work. I used to say to myself that I am only 2 per cent better than an average club fullback:1 per cent = experience

1 per cent = effort in preparation; during the game I knew if I ever dropped my effort on the latter then I would become an average club fullback.

The question is – who do you compete against in training? If you are only running fast enough to beat the next fastest player on your club team, that defines your limit. Somewhere in the country, I knew there was a full forward training and improving. I used to picture him and race against him in my head at training.

This extends off the football pitch. There is a saying that 'you're the average of the five people you spend the most time with'. The people you surround yourself with are going to define your limits. They will either empower and support you or drain energy and focus from you. The great thing is that you can decide who you spend time with. You can seek out progressive people and drift away from the negative.

I was part of successful minor and u21 Mayo teams from 2005 to 2008. At the time there was limited social media. Traditional media was run by reputable local journalists that wouldn't criticise such a young player. All the reports were great and stoked my ego. I became addicted to reading about how great I was. In 2009 I started playing senior football. All of a sudden, I was fair game for criticism in traditional media and trolls started appearing on social media. It took years to wean myself off the need for external validation. If I was to re-do my whole career, I would have ignored it in my early days. If you can't stomach the bad reports then you can't rely on the good ones.

These two matches and how I handled them stand out in my memory. I played in a Minor All-Ireland final in 2005. We got routed by Down in the first half. I was one of the leaders on the team and decided I was going to single-handedly bring us back into the game. I intercepted a pass in our fullback line and took off on an inspirational run through four Down forwards. Of course I was pulled up for over carrying and the rout continued.

My first championship start of the 2011 season was against Cork in the All-Ireland quarter final. My first involvement was to give away a penalty. I knew at that point that I wasn't going to get a man of the match award today. Instead I focused on having a 'good shitty day'. I didn't over-commit in any tackles, I got my hands on the ball and gave a simple hand pass, I built myself back into the game. We didn't concede a score in the second half.

Also – don't bring white towels to training.

James Barry
TIPPERARY HURLER 2014-2019

Barry enjoyed success in his underage career, winning minor and u21 Munster and All-Ireland titles. However, Barry didn't walk straight into the senior squad, but he was a key part of the Premier County's All-Ireland Intermediate success in 2012. The 2016 All-Star also won back-to-back Fitzgibbons with UCC in 2012 and 2013, and two All-Irelands in 2016 and 2019.

Doing the right amount of preparation is so important no matter what you are doing in life, whether it's school, work or sports. The type and amount of preparation you do will dictate how you perform in your chosen field.

Any athlete or business person who is successful in life has spent a huge amount of time and effort preparing their skills; whether it's free taking, giving presentations or even sitting an exam, you have to put in the time beforehand to make sure you succeed. Putting in the time for preparation is never easy, but when you do finally succeed at what you are trying to achieve it will be worth it.

Bríd Stack
CORK FOOTBALLER 2004-2018

Stack is one of the most successful footballers to ever play the game, one of only four players to have tallied eleven senior All-Ireland medals and played every minute of every final in which she and Cork were successful. She also won eleven National Leagues, Footballer of the year in 2016 and was nominated for RTÉ Sportsperson of the year in the same year. She has recently signed for the GWS Giants in the AFLW.

Dear Future Star,

There are a few things that you have no control over. The bus was late so now you're late, the teacher you really wanted for Leaving Cert Maths is going on maternity leave and God help us when your friend likes the same person that you do.

Thankfully, there is plenty that you can control and secondary school is where you are first tested. You have complete control over your effort, your attitude, your dedication, your patience, your motivation and who you choose to surround yourself with. Effectively, you are in control of your own choices. So what is it that you really want?

When I started secondary school, I did so with two other girls from my primary school. Unfortunately for me, on our first day, the two girls did their own thing so I had to look after myself. I launched myself into sport. I had played football and badminton in primary school and felt really comfortable with them, but I also decided to take up basketball as I had never played it before. Sport has that remarkable way of bringing likeminded people together and within my first month of school I had a fabulous group of new and exciting friends.

By Leaving Cert, I was training three times a week with school teams, twice a week with club football, Cork training three times a week and then matches most weekends. I made sure I never missed a training session; I didn't want to anyway. I loved the freedom that sport gave me and I felt I studied better after getting out for an hour. When travelling to games, I only ever brought one piece of work as anything more was futile for me. I made sure I focused on that one thing, like an Irish essay, and knew it well by the time I got home. I always found out what I had missed in classes and essentially, I guess, I tried to make the most effective use of my time. I understand there are more distractions nowadays; YouTubers weren't really big when I was in secondary school. Instagram scrolling didn't cost you a day of your life, but I still had to make choices for what I valued most. I valued my family, my friends, my sport and doing well in the Leaving. Time management, organisation and good sleep patterns were vital for me and they will be vital for you if you want to find balance. Keep asking yourself, what is it you really want to achieve and work towards that.

The main things I have gotten from sport are quantifiable. Firstly, sport has given me a sense of belonging that some people search their whole lives to find. I am so thankful for my involvement in team sports as I have a circle of truly sincere friends that I have been lucky to know for well over ten years. We were introduced through our common interest in football, but what has developed is so much more. We have been there for each other through good times and bad, through family losses and new additions, we can share our weaknesses and we can celebrate our strengths together. Most importantly we are completely comfortable in each other's company, safe in the knowledge that there is always a loyal and listening ear if it is ever needed. Through playing for each other on the sporting field, we have developed friendships that are backboned by trust and mutual respect.

Sport has always made me identify the honesty of my efforts. If I didn't put in a wholehearted effort, then why should I feel entitled to success? This is also true for exam results. You can have results, or you can have excuses, but you can't have both.

Sport has helped me to become disciplined. Every sport has rules just like so many facets of life. If you can't abide by the rules then things aren't going to work out for you. In terms of health, it has definitely made me realise the importance of keeping fit and healthy. I am at my happiest when I am at my fittest. When I eat well and exercise, I look better and then I feel better. Being healthy has a knock-on effect and will have a big say in your mental health and happiness.

My parting words to you would be – Choose to make physical activity an integral part of your life. Don't give up on sport just because you had one bad experience or because you didn't like the trainer or because your friends aren't doing it anymore. You will be faced with many obstacles in life and I feel sport has taught me vital coping skills that I can draw on when things don't always work out. And believe me, they won't always work out. You may not like team sports. You may not like competitive sport. But one thing's for certain, there's a sport or an activity out there for everyone's ability. So go try out tag rugby, do a parkrun with a friend, go to an exercise class – find what appeals to you.

I am eternally grateful that I got involved in sport. It has made my character stronger and my life fuller. So don't be afraid to try something new because it's scary and you might fail. Don't be a sheep and follow the crowd. Don't be lazy. Always be true to yourself and always be honest with yourself.

Get out, get active and get a little bit happier every time you do.

Yours in Sport,
Bríd Stack

Aidan O'Mahony
KERRY FOOTBALLER 2004-2017

Following Kerry's All-Ireland semi-final defeat to Tyrone in 2003, it was clear that the Kingdom lacked edge and physicality in their defence. These are traits that O'Mahony brought to his game every time he took to the pitch. A no-nonsense defender, he won three National Leagues, ten Munster titles, five All-Irelands, and two All-Star awards.

I started my career when there was no gym work and most of training consisted of running and skills. Fast forward to now and it's all about getting balance between gym work and pitch. At the end of the day the game is still about skills!

I'm fortunate that I've been involved with young kids in development squads and what I always look out for are players who want to learn. They don't have to be the most skilful or quickest. They just need to show they want to be there, they want to learn and then you watch them grow every week as they work on skills as well as learning how to be a team player.

In terms of gym work for young people, you need to do the same movement in the gym that you are using on the pitch! For me the gym needs to be all about mobility and movement, body-weight exercises are just as good as any weight you will lift! For any team sport you play now it's all about getting conditioned in the off season and preparation for your pre-season!. The best players are not the players who lift the most in the gym, they are the players who practise their skills the most, they always have a ball in their hands and always strive to be better!

We are now living in a generation where there is so much information out there for players and fitness is the new social scene. Enjoy it, get out and train; healthy body = healthy mind.

Eoghan O'Donnell
DUBLIN HURLER 2016-PRESENT

One of the country's top man-markers. O'Donnell enjoyed a successful underage career winning minor and u21 Leinster titles, while also being selected for the 2016 u21 Team of the Year. The 2019 All-Star nominee has been at the heart of the Dublin defence, generally picking up the opposition's talisman.

The Strength of the GAA

This is a piece that is close to my heart as I was born in Botswana and lived in Zimbabwe until I was six years old. Moving to Ireland was very challenging in a number of ways. The weather was different, the schools, food and people were different and the culture of Ireland itself was difficult to adapt to as a child. To say I was homesick was an understatement and I felt that way until I was introduced to the GAA. A flier came in through the door for my local club, Whitehall Colmcilles, for nursery training on Saturday morning. My dad brought me up that morning with a new helmet and hurl and I haven't looked back since.

The GAA has been a core part of my life since I was six years old, from training twice a week with a match on the weekend all through my underage days to now training four or five times a week with the Dublin senior hurlers. As with the majority of people that play hurling or football, the friends I made with the club were also the same people I went to primary and secondary school with. These friends I made playing up through the ages of Whitehall are some of my closest friends today. The community atmosphere of the GAA is so unique to Ireland that it makes us feel part of something special. Being the strongest, fastest or best player can be great, but it is the friendships and sense of belonging that sticks with us most as we get older. It is for these reasons that I am proud to be part of the GAA.

Finally, to all aspiring young boys and girls who want to improve their skills and represent their club and hopefully someday their county. The best bit of advice I can give is to try to find balance in your approach to training and practice. People can get the idea that to be successful you have to train hard every single day and sacrifice fun. The more enjoyable you can make your experience the more you will thrive in it. Try to make it social by meeting your friends at your local GAA pitch and pucking in groups rather than trying to train every day by yourself. Even if it is only walking to the shop, try to bring your hurls and puck away together, this will improve your touch massively! Try to find balance in the food you eat too, don't cut out the Mars bars and pizzas completely, just limit them to treats while eating a good breakfast, lunch and dinner most days. The last balance you have to find is with your strength and conditioning. My advice on this is to listen to your coaches and look for advice before getting into gym programmes, especially for underage players. If you can find balance across all these, you're giving yourself the best chance to represent your club and your county in the future.

Neil Patrick Collins
ROSCOMMON FOOTBALLER 2012-2016

Collins was a key part of the Rossies' defence during his time with them. He won a National League in 2015. In 2018 Collins transferred to New York, nearly defeating Leitrim to give the Exiles a first Connacht championship victory.

Nutrition

Nutritional choices and practice are varying dependent on each individual, and it is the responsibility of each of us to figure out what our own bodies respond well to, or not. For me, cutting down significantly on dairy products and wheat has me feeling more energised and lighter than before. Over the years, I would feel a lethargy and heaviness on myself when I made the wrong food choices, so now I ensure I only eat quality meals which controls this for the most part. Usually a breakfast would be a fresh, healthy one consisting of fruits (blueberries, oranges, strawberries, and banana) ,an omelette and a piece or two of wholemeal bread. Dinners are usually heavy on the vegetable side with a high quality, lean meat preferably. I noticed a huge difference in my energy when I began buying organic foods. I eat quite a lot of vegan food, although I am not vegan myself. I feel light, energetic and clear minded after most vegan meals I eat.

I definitely like a biscuit or two with a cup of tea in the evenings, so that would be my advice.

Gym

Again, the gym depends on the specific goals of the person. Whenever I trained heavy in the gym, I wasn't as light on my feet as would have been ideal, so in the key moments of the year there would be very little lifting and more so light activation and body weight exercise. The strength will never leave once you have spent time building it, so to be as light and fast on the feet as possible would also have been my aim. I found a big difference in my overall health when I stretched consistently. To be strong but light is the aim.

Skill

Spending time on the weaker side of the body (in my case the left-hand side) not only improves that side, but also improves the strong side as the body becomes more balanced. This takes time and patience. For me, I used to kick only on my left in the early parts of training sessions, which over time made me so much more accomplished in my skillset. Also, I like doing keepie-uppies, which improve a person's touch with their feet. Just balancing and having fun with a ball can lead to huge improvements over time.

Mindset

For me, mindset is incredibly difficult to master, but ultimately the basics are simple. Mindset in theory is straightforward, but to practise it requires constant awareness and control over the subconscious brain. To see yourself as being the best in your position and in your role. To see yourself in the best possible way, emphasising your strengths and powers. To focus only on what you can control. And to earn your own respect. To value and love yourself and believe thoroughly in achieving whatever it is you want.

Lifestyle Preparation

For me, to be happy in my life is to be successful. Happiness off the field equates to enjoyment and full expression on it. So to be true to myself, understand myself and allow that to shine, doing what I believe in and enjoy. That is my lifestyle preparation.

Advice to younger self

Being positive in the way I see myself and my place in the world would be the best thing I could teach my younger self. To see myself as a powerful person with a unique viewpoint and voice. To trust myself and my instincts thoroughly and fully. To have compassion towards myself for the things I am not so good at. It would be to look inside rather than looking outside, with love and respect.

Paul Curran
TIPPERARY HURLER 2001-2015

A driving-force both on and off the pitch, Curran was a key part of the Premier County's successes during his lengthy career. A dual player at minor, he won a Munster Minor Hurling Championship. He retired with a medal haul of two Fitzgibbons with WIT, two National Leagues, four Munster Championships and an All-Ireland. The two-time All-Star has also won a Tipperary SHC with his club, Mullinahone.

Advice to my younger self

You are more than just a hurler/footballer/sports person. Of course, whatever sport you participate in, commit to it fully, train hard, make the necessary sacrifices required to be the best that you can be. But remember sport doesn't, and should not, define you, it can be a big part of your life, but don't let it consume you. It's imperative that you realise the importance of expanding and investing in other areas of your life, be it academically, be it nurturing family relationships or simply pursuing various other interests and hobbies. This is a far healthier mindset and approach to follow and it will result in a more rounded individual with plenty of options open to them when their sports career comes to a conclusion.

It's also important to bring a curious mindset, seek out help and advice early on in your career from people you value and respect. Search for a mentor or mentors who can provide you with guidance and assistance along your journey. Realise that you are on a journey, savour and enjoy it and most importantly don't limit yourself.

Sinéad Finnegan
DUBLIN FOOTBALLER 2005-2019

A true leader and communicator at the back, Finnegan showed time and time again to be one of the finest defenders in the country, lining out at both full and centre back throughout her career. Her honours include a National League, twelve Leinster Championships, four All-Irelands and an All-Star in 2015.

Nutrition

When I was growing up, I suppose nutrition wasn't something that I would have put a massive emphasis on, but now that I'm older, I realise good nutrition can have an impact on how you play, your energy levels, your mood, your ability to recovery from an injury or even prevent you from getting injured.

I think the biggest barrier to good nutrition is lack of organisation, so in order to eat well you need to prepare well! I used to work in a really busy job and between it and training I had very little time to prepare my food. This led to me:

1. Not eating enough food to have enough energy to train at the best of my ability;

2. Eating poorer foods that I would not have chosen had I the time to prepare correctly.

I was constantly tired and picking up small injuries which was very frustrating. So, I needed to become more organised if I wanted to continue playing at a high level. Sometimes I would have skipped breakfast so I made a rule that this was no longer happening. I would either make overnight oats the day before (these are so quick and easy) or have a slice of brown bread with scrambled eggs, spinach and baked ham. Again, that seems like an effort, but it is made in the microwave in work in three minutes and was so tasty too. On days where I wasn't training I would simply have yoghurt with raspberries, cinnamon and flaxseed in the morning. For my main meals I would spend time at the weekend batch cooking, making things like curries or a chicken bake and storing them in the freezer, so I didn't have to spend time cooking every day. I would usually eat my dinner at lunch time and have something smaller in the evening. This could be an omelette (if I hadn't had any eggs for breakfast that morning).

It's not that you never put a bar of chocolate in your mouth again! Of course you can and of course I do! It's about trying to eat well 80 per cent of the time, to give yourself the best chance to be ready and able to play. If you have a real sweet tooth though, there are loads of recipes out there for delicious but healthy treats – I love the food flicker chocolate protein bars!

Preparation

Preparation is a very individual thing, so I'll tell you what I do, but others will have a different approach.

The day before a game I will get up early and enjoy a big breakfast, usually banana oat pancakes with yoghurt, raspberries, cinnamon, flaxseed, nuts and some honey on top. If it's sunny outside I will sit outside and eat it out there, and sometimes one of my teammates who lives close by would call over to have pancakes with me. After that I will sit up in my bed and analyse the opponent; I spend time looking at the overall team, but as a back I would put more focus on the opponents' forward line and specifically my player if I know who I'm marking. I know it's not realistic for everyone to be able to do that, but if you are playing a team that you have played before, it's good to have a think about how they play, the feet they kick with. I usually spend about an hour to two hours doing that. I will then write down some points that I have taken away from studying the opposition and set targets for myself for the game – so this could be something along the lines of, I want to get three blocks, six turnovers and a catch above my head. I write down about three points; it's useful for looking back on after a game to see whether you met what you wanted to achieve. Then it's time to eat again. I would usually have something like soup and a chicken sandwich, and make sure I'm drinking water throughout the day. I then make sure my football gear is washed, and if not, I'll put it in the wash. Then I'll usually try and keep myself busy for the day up until about 6 pm; visit friends or family, go for a walk, watch a movie, go shopping, anything like that that keeps my mind off the game. Then it's time for dinner and while I'm cooking I would pack my bag for the game and then just chill for the evening. I'd go to bed usually at 10.30pm. The morning of the game is very relaxed because I will have everything organised the day before.

I suppose for preparation I would say (particularly if it's a big game) it is important to have a think about your opponents and how you'd like to play, but after you've done that it's good to stop thinking about it and just trust that you're ready and go and enjoy the game! I know that if I've spent time looking into who I'm playing against, I will go out onto the pitch a much more confident player.

Diarmuid O'Sullivan
CORK HURLER 1997-2009

Some might say where the stereotypes of fullbacks come from, 'The Rock' was a key part of Cork's success during a golden era for the Leesiders. His first taste of success at county level came at u21, winning two Munster titles and two All-Irelands. He was named Young Hurler of the Year in 1999. During his time with the rebels he won a National League, five Munster Championships and three All-Irelands. The four-time All-Star has also achieved club success, winning a Cork IHC and Cork SHC with Cloyne and Imokilly respectively. The Rock also represented the Rebels in football, winning Munster championships at both junior and senior level. He is currently a selector with the county's hurlers.

How do you get rid of nerves before a game?

Some people think nerves are a myth. How do you deal with them? When I was playing, we used to keep a training log of what we did over the course of a season: good things, bad things, positive things, negative things. Always coming up to a game you'd reflect back to your little notebook and tick off your checklist and say, 'Yeah I've my hurling done, my first touch is good, my speed work is done, my strength and conditioning is done.' You just revert back to your little black book, your sacred book that gives you the confidence as a player, knowing you have the work done because you can read back over weeks and weeks of work from the start of the season and it just gives you the confidence.

Coming up to big games myself, what helped with nerves was a reassurance that I could go back, look at my notebook and say 'Yeah, I have x, y and z done.' From this I knew I was happy going onto the field with all my boxes ticked.

Other guys have different rituals and different bits and pieces for how they deal with nerves. Some guys like to put on their music, other guys like to sit in the corner and be quiet. They're the guys you tend to worry about as a coach, the guys who are a bit withdrawn from the group and are a bit quieter, because they're the guys who are suffering the most. You make sure either yourself, another player or a part of the management team will go to him and acknowledge their journey and how they've come from the training ground to championship day. Just give them reassurance.

I think that any positive you can give a player going into a big game is always beneficial. No matter how small or how meaningless you think a little word can be to a player, it can be a big thing and settle all the nerves.

Obviously when you get onto the field, you go through your warmup routine, that's another avenue for it. One that can really settle players down is when you contest your first possession in a game, if you get a comfortable possession early on, you're going to be very confident straight away. It'll just flow after that.

What's the best way to mark someone?

You'll always come up against someone who will be that bit quicker, who might be that bit taller, who might be a better hurler than you. It's very, very important you do your homework before the game, so Seán O'Sullivan might be quicker than me, but he always likes to turn on his left hand, if I turn him to his right side where I know he's uncomfortable, that's a win for me. I will take away his speed if I can turn him that way. If he's taller than me, how do I stop that? By keeping the ball out of his hand, by competing and forcing him to fight for the breaks on the ground.

You do your homework. I suppose it was starting to come into the game towards the end of my inter-county career. I know a lot of players do it now, they're looking at videos of their direct opponents and analysing them in minute detail to the point where they know everything about everyone they could be marking.

You have a mental database built up on each guy you might be marking. Say if you were going out and playing against Aaron Gillane on Sunday, what does Aaron like to do? If you were out against one of the Bennetts or Tadhg de Búrca, what are their strengths? You analyse their strengths and weaknesses, to give yourself a small bit of an advantage. They might be quicker or stronger, but then you think of your own positives and how you can counteract that.

What's the best advice you were given during your career?

I'd always revert back to one that I probably still religiously live by - do the simple things well and you will get better at them i.e. catching, striking off your left, right, picking the ball up, hooking, blocking and flicking. I fully believe they're the fundamentals of the game. You do the simple things well and everything will flow after that. I was always told to concentrate on the fundamentals and when you can tick that box of doing all those things right, that will allow you to express yourself and play hurling with the freedom of knowing you can execute these skills at a high level, high speed, and high intensity in the biggest games you'll ever play.

What was the biggest change you had to make to your own game during your career?

When I first started playing inter-county, I was only young, just nineteen years of age playing senior hurling championship. The game was different, you looked after your own space, you cleared your own ball and you got it as far away from the goal as possible. There was no such thing as playing to systems, playing through the lines etc. You looked after your own corner, and when you had your own corner looked after, you looked after the guy beside you if he needed help.

I suppose the biggest change was when the game started to move on and develop. In Cork it was the 2003/04 season when we started to play a more possession-based game, where there was a lot more responsibility put on us to look after the ball, to use the ball shorter, to give the ball to the guy in the best position, when you give it you go again and get it off his shoulder.

That was probably the first insight we had into modern era hurling. It did take a while, because if you're playing from a young age that you win your own ball, you drive it down the field to the forwards, the forward wins his own ball and maybe tries to put it over the bar. It was the start of an evolution for us in Cork.

It was mindset. Okay, the rationale was there which was put to us, it was just the mindset of how to get there and how to do it. It was a great challenge. I remember Dónal O'Grady and his management team at the time, they challenged us to change, because we had all played a similar type of game from minor and u21. We were successful at the older type of game in '99 but lost a bit of ground before Dónal came in. When he came in he said we needed to change and that was probably the hardest thing. We had to change; in respect of possession and to use the ball really well and intelligently for the next couple of years after that.

What are County Panels looking for?

I'd be of the opinion that you don't need to be the most talented guy in the group. You want guys who are coachable.

It's the guy who's willing to come in and give an 8/10, 9/10 performance at training every night. They're the type of guys they're looking for, sure you won't get it every night. It's the guys who are constantly looking to improve, wanting to learn and constantly looking for video analysis. They're the type of player you need, they're the type of players you want because that's the level the game has gone to. It's not just turn up and train anymore, it's the guy who you know will do his recovery on a Wednesday morning after a hard session on the Tuesday. He'll do his video analysis work coming up to the weekend of a game, it's the guy who'll have his gym session in the bag. If they have that eagerness to learn, you've got one hell of a player on your hands.

The player is changing. It's not just show up and train and play anymore. There's so much more, you have the technical side of it, skill, the strength and conditioning side of it, but I think one of the biggest changes in the game now is time management. We have guys who are in college, guys who are working and constantly trying to find that balance between work, life, training, college and it's difficult to try and marry them all up. It's guys who are going to dedicate themselves to that routine that we're looking for. He doesn't have to be the most skilful. You can improve, and you'll improve because your work ethic is good along with your hunger and willingness to learn. Your hurling will get better when you come into that environment – but it's guys who are willing to dedicate themselves to get better on an individual basis and get better as a collective with the group over a period of time.

Cathal McCarron
TYRONE FOOTBALLER 2008-2018

Following an All-Ireland success in his breakout year, McCarron went on to enjoy further success with the Red Hand, winning three Ulster titles and picking up three All-Star nominations in 2013,2015 and 2016. He has also had success with his club, Dromore St Dympna's, winning three Tyrone championships before transferring to Athy.

If I was to do it all again, I would say self-care is so important during your teenage years and early adulthood. Just looking after yourself mentally and dealing with the challenges that life presents. Happily, in recent years opening up to friends and family about problems has come to be seen as a strength and not a weakness. Opening up to others and looking after the mental side of life will bring your football career to places you can only dream of.

On the pitch and off it, I would say hard work, pure hard work and dedication got my football career to the levels that I can be proud of. I can say I have no regrets and I loved every minute of it. Cherish the good times and learn from the tough times.

Paddy Stapleton

TIPPERARY HURLER 2006-2016

Stapleton fulfilled a lifelong dream when he was brought into the Tipperary Senior squad by Babs Keating in 2006. Over the next ten years he enjoyed a rake of success with the Premier County, winning minor and u21 Munster titles, six Munster Titles, a National League and two All-Irelands. Stapleton was also nominated for an All-Star on three occasions in 2009, 2010 and 2014. He has also won a Tipperary SHC and a Munster Club Championship with Borrisoleigh.

Practice

No doubt you will have heard it a million times – 'practice makes perfect'. Unfortunately, there is no way around it, if you want to improve at anything in life you are going to have to do it until it is as natural as tying your shoelaces. When you started out at the shoelaces it seemed like you didn't know your bunny ears from your hoops and loops, but now I'm sure you could do it while reciting the alphabet backwards. The only other tip is that really it should be, '*proper* practice makes perfect'. Watch the best players, the ones that do all the simple skills consistently and steal parts of their game. Maybe it's Daithí Burke as a back, or TJ Reid in the forwards, what are the things they do well? Then go practise them. Yes, they can do all the difficult things like sidelines and shooting on the back foot, but it is the rising, striking, catching and tackling that you will use the majority of the time on the pitch so practise them until you get them right 99 per cent of the time. After all, no one is perfect.

Improvement

I see a lot of kids with great potential at u10, u12 and u14 levels but they often fall by the wayside as they grow up. A lot of the time it is because they ignore the weaknesses in their game or ignore a coach who encourages them to improve. I'm thinking of a kid who has great speed, but never improves their passing. A child who has a massive strike standing still, but will not challenge themselves by striking on the run. Someone who only thinks that they are in the forwards to score, but doesn't think about working so hard that they dispossess their opponent. You need to keep working hard on your strengths, but if you ignore your weaknesses, you will find it difficult to compete at a higher level. Try to look at your own abilities with a clear vision – there is always something to improve.

Strong mind

If you are striving to improve as discussed above then you are doing the hardest part. The other side of things is in your head. If you are working hard at your game and giving your all in matches then you will always improve. Some players are like Austin Gleeson and Noel McGrath, made for the big stage and arrive at a very early age, while others take some more time to develop. It is usually a bumpy road, but that makes it all the sweeter when you finally realise your ambitions. The only chance you have is if you keep your attitude strong while you practise, train and play to improve all the time. No one can guarantee where you will end up, but having a good work ethic and attitude is your best chance to fulfil your dreams.

Leah Caffrey
DUBLIN FOOTBALLER 2013-PRESENT

Following success at minor winning an All-Ireland, Caffrey was called in to the Jackies' senior squad. She later won two All-Irelands at u21 level. She was a key part of Dublin's recent success winning two National Leagues and three All-Irelands. The two-time All-Star has also won two Dublin SFC and a Leinster Club Championship with her club, Na Fianna.

What has your experience in the gym taught you?

I was first introduced to the gym when I was minor. I didn't know what I was doing. When I joined the senior team and saw the standard of the older girls in the gym, I realised I had a lot to learn. Progress in the gym can take time so I think it's important to have patience with yourself. As the standard of ladies' football is improving, strength and conditioning is becoming more and more important. Even though it is said to be a 'non-contact sport' there is plenty of physicality, and to avoid injuries in games, it's important to focus on this part of your game.

How do you look after your nutrition?

I try to eat well 80 per cent of the time and allow the other 20 per cent for treats. When we are training, I would focus on eating carbohydrates before and recovering after with carbohydrates and protein. On rest days I would look to get lots of fruit and veg into my diet. On match days I would base my meals on carbohydrate options, like banana pancakes.

How do you find football impacts your lifestyle?

Football demands a lot, but is also very rewarding. It is full on, but you also make great friends, learn a few lessons and make great memories.

How important is preparation for you?

I'm quite bad at prep before a game and I'm usually very last-minute, but having my bag packed the night before and planning my meals for the following day help me to relax before a big game. It just doesn't happen too often!

What advice would you give to your younger self?

Keep practising, use your instep and appreciate the support your coaches and parents offer.

Pamela Mackey
CORK CAMOGIE PLAYER 2009-PRESENT

One of Cork's most consistent defenders over the past decade. A four-time All-Star, Mackey, through her speed and attacking attributes, has often turned defence into attack for the Leesiders. A player whose work rate and talent is never found wanting when the pressure is on, she has won a National League and five All-Irelands during her time with the Rebelettes. She has also won two Cork Senior Camogie Championships with her club, Douglas.

At the highest level, in sport and in life, you are always going to meet people who are more talented than you, but talent only gets you so far. Success is achieved through hard work and persistence. To get the best out of yourself and fulfil your potential you must be willing to work on all aspects of your game, so don't be afraid to challenge yourself and step outside your comfort zone.

Gym and lifestyle
A good pre-season in the gym is not only key for injury prevention, it also presents an excellent opportunity to vary your training and work on your weaknesses. Additionally, self-discipline and commitment outside of team training is essential. Always be prepared to go that extra mile whether that is going to the ball-alley to work on your skills or going to the sea for some recovery.

Mental preparation
If you want to take your game to the next level, putting time and effort into your mental preparation is key. When you're a young athlete this can often be neglected. In the heat of battle during a big game more often than not it comes down to whether you can control the negative thoughts and emotions which have a huge impact on performance. Visualisation, main-

taining a positive self-image and preparing a mistake strategy can really improve your performance level.

Nutrition

With regards to nutrition, maintaining a healthy diet consistently can be more difficult for some people than others. In this regard, my advice would be to try and experiment with different types of food. It doesn't have to be as boring as chicken, broccoli and rice!

Advice to my younger self

Be an individual, don't conform to the stereotype just because everyone else around you does. Stay true to your moral values and principles. When you're younger, a lot of us say I'd be happy if I had wealth, if I had these attributes but true happiness comes from deep inside. Finally, the best piece of advice I can give is to accept yourself unconditionally for who you are. Remember 'The greatest victory is over yourself, it's always too soon to quit!'

Keith Higgins
MAYO FOOTBALLER 2006-2021

For well over a decade, Higgins has proved time and time again why he was one of the country's tightest defenders. He has also shown great versatility, playing at centre forward during the 2013 season. Zippy has also lined out for the county's hurlers. His honours include a Sigerson, u21 Connacht, u21 All-Ireland, eight Connacht titles, Young Footballer of the Year 2006 and four All-Stars. He also won a Nicky Rackard Cup in 2016 with Mayo's hurlers and has taken over the captaincy for 2021.

Gym

I have to admit I was probably a bit behind everyone else when it came to fully utilising the benefits of good strength and conditioning. But it definitely has had huge benefits for me in terms of core strength and injury prevention, especially over the last three or four years. For me, the gym work has never been about putting on lots of muscle, it was more about getting good core strength and maintaining that explosive power which I feel really added to speed on the pitch, which was an important part of how I play. But I would advise any young players out there if they are doing gym work to seek proper help and get the right type of programme especially starting off.

Nutrition

Again, there are massive gains to be had by athletes who look after their nutrition and put a focus on getting the right fuels into their bodies to help perform. But again, for any younger players starting off I would always keep it simple: get good foods into you, hydrate and don't skip meals.

Lifestyle

For me, lifestyle is a choice any athlete has to make if they are serious about trying to become the best at their chosen sport. Gym, nutrition, sleep all fall under the heading of lifestyle and doing the right thing to make sure it helps you get better is the biggest choice. However, I also feel that balance is very important and players need to have that balance right between their sport, school, job, family life etc. If you are happy in what you are doing off the pitch it will be easier to be happy on the pitch.

Skill Development

Again, skill development is fundamental to any sport and the only way this gets better is through putting in the time and practice. Identify areas you need to work on and don't be afraid to ask coaches for areas they feel you need to improve. Get the basics right and everything else will follow, but also don't neglect the things you are good at. They also continue to need work.

Ken McGrath

Kevin Cassidy

Tommy Walsh

Elaine O'Meara

THE HALFBACKS' ADVICE

Aaron Kernan

Tiernan McCann

Tommy Walsh
KILKENNY HURLER 2002-2014

One of the greatest to ever grace Croke Park, Walsh defined versatility, winning All-Stars at corner-back, half-back, midfield and half-forward. The Cats legend won a Leinster Minor title, two u21 Leinster titles, two u21 All-Irelands, seven National Leagues, nine Leinster titles, nine All-Irelands, nine All-Stars in a row and was named the 2009 Hurler of the Year. Following his retirement with Kilkenny, Walsh has gone on to win a Kilkenny Intermediate Championship, Leinster Intermediate Championship and All-Ireland Club Championship with Tullaroan.

Enjoyment

It is important to enjoy your sport. Keep this at the back of your mind at all times. Focus on the areas you enjoy and work and work and work to improve those areas. You will find as you work hard on an area and if you see improvement, great feelings of satisfaction will follow.

Spirit

It is hugely rewarding to throw yourself into a team environment. When you play with a group of your teammates, you win some and you lose some, but if you do your best to focus on a spirit that brings you all together, the times you play and train will be some of the most enjoyable days of your life.

Focus on You

Don't compare yourself to others. Whatever your chosen sport, you will need to learn the basics, but after acquiring the basics you should work hard on your own strengths. Yes, it will be natural you want to be the best and if that is your goal don't let anybody change your mind. Focus on what you are good at and work your socks off to become better.

Winning

Winning. Enjoy the wins. I often hear people at the end of their careers discuss how they regret not enjoying their wins more. When you practise and train hard, it is a great feeling when you win and you deserve to enjoy it.

Eoin Murchan
DUBLIN FOOTBALLER 2017-PRESENT

One of the fastest players in the country, Murchan has shown he is more than capable of balancing attack and defence, scoring the crucial goal that sealed Dublin's five-in-a-row success, while also generally picking up the opposition's linkman. A key part of the Dubs u21 Leinster and All-Ireland Championship successes in 2017, he made his debut with the seniors later that season. Since then he has won a National League, three Leinster Championships, three All-Irelands and an All-Star. He has also won a Dublin Minor Championship and a Dublin u21 Championship with Na Fianna.

How do I gain confidence on the pitch?

If you have the basic skills of Gaelic football down it makes everything else a lot easier. Concentrate on improving the fundamentals of your game before worrying about any other aspects.

What is the most important thing in preparing for a game?

The key to preparing for a game is to get a proper night's sleep in before a game. For me that means having my bag prepared the evening before with everything I need so I don't have to worry about it.

How old were you when you knew you wanted to play for Dublin?

I'm not sure, I remember going to see Dublin play in Croke Park as a boy and looking up to some of those players. But I was lucky enough to play a few different sports and loved them all so Gaelic wasn't my sole focus, which was definitely a good thing.

What is the most important sporting lesson you have had to learn?

There are going to be as many setbacks as high points. There are always going to be losses that stick with you and injury setbacks, but it's about learning from these experiences to better yourself.

Ryan McHugh
DONEGAL FOOTBALLER 2013-PRESENT

Donegal's linkman, McHugh has been a key part of the Ulster men's success in recent seasons. The 2014 Young Footballer of the Year has an impressive haul of awards and medals with three Ulster titles and two All-Stars in 2016 and 2018, one in the halfback line the other in the half-forward line.

Skill Development

I believe to improve your skill you have to practise and practise a lot. Growing up, I spent a lot of time practising to be able to kick as well off my left foot as I can off my right foot. I always tried to go to my local club pitch and practise my shooting as much as possible and I believe this has helped a lot. You will never be the finished product, but if you practise enough and train hard you will be the best you can be.

Brendan Bugler
CLARE HURLER 2007-2017

A two-time All-Star, Bugler always played with passion. A vital pillar in the Banner's All-Ireland success in 2013, he has also won a Fitzgibbon with UL and two

National Leagues. With his club, Whitegate he has won two Clare Intermediate Championships. Bugler has previously worked as a member of Davy Fitzgerald's Wexford backroom team as a forwards' coach.

Nutrition

Our S&C coach/dietician Joe O'Connor always said to eat the colours of the rainbow, every single day. Make sure you get your fruits, carbohydrates, fats and proteins in.

Strength and Conditioning

One of the areas that went through the most change during my time with Clare. When I started on the panel, we'd only do gym work for a couple of months up until the league started, any muscle that we'd have built up would be gone come championship. As the years went on the role of S&C coach became more important. We used to do gym sessions throughout the year with the bulk of it being done in pre-season and it was all about maintaining it during the season. The schedule would have been Monday gym, Tuesday field session, Wednesday rest, Thursday gym, Friday field session, Saturday rest and Sunday field session or a match.

What are county panels looking for?

The most important characteristic I look for in a player is attitude, they have got to be coachable. I've seen many players who have had bags of talent at underage, but the wrong attitude. They weren't coachable and didn't fulfil their potential. I've also seen the opposite, players with excellent attitudes, the growth mindset, always looking to grow, always willing to learn and I've seen them go on to be top inter-county hurlers. Treat every day like a learning day.

Secondly, you need to have the utmost dedication. If you want to play at the top level, if you want to be an elite sportsperson, you have got to stand out from the crowd when it comes to your dedication. There are choices you have to make as you grow older, some people call them sacrifices. They're not sacrifices if you use them to fulfil your full potential and be the best you can be.

Tiernan McCann
TYRONE FOOTBALLER 2014-PRESENT

Starting his career off with the Red Hand in the half-forward line, his move to half-back saw him thrive in this new role. Since then McCann has proven to be one of the top attacking half-backs around picking up two Ulster titles and All-Star nominations in 2017 and 2018. He has also won a Tyrone SFC with his club Killyclogher St Mary's.

Setbacks

We all encounter setbacks in our lives, whether they arise in our sporting, educational, professional or personal life. They can hit when you least expect it and for many they come at the worst times. With any setback there may be an array of emotional states associated. Why me? Why now? What did I do to deserve this? The initial period of suffering a bump in the road may leave us feeling fragile, alone, dejected, demotivated, worried, and afraid. I would encourage people to focus on positive thinking. Use the setback as a springboard to propel yourself forward. Use it as a motivating tool for yourself:

'I can come back stronger from this; I will come back stronger than ever before.'

Fall down seven times stand up eight.

Elaine O'Meara

DUBLIN CAMOGIE PLAYER 2005-2016

A key part of the Dublin team that won back-to-back Junior All-Irelands in 2005 and 2006, O'Meara was called up to the Jackies' first team, where she played a key role in defence over the next eleven seasons. The former Dublin captain has also won a Dublin Championship with her club, Na Fianna.

I love camogie, I always have. When I was young I asked my dad to bring me training because I was jealous of my brother getting to go and not me. And once I was brought that was it. If I was told to be somewhere for training or a match, I was there. You just went – it wasn't an option. You have decided to play, you love playing, so you go. No time for excuses. I made it onto the Dublin panel in 2005 and played pretty much full on for the next eleven years.

One of the main things I learnt is that it takes more than skill to be part of an inter-county set up for that long. It's down to attitude and those extra miles that you are willing to go for your team. I was never the 'best player' on the team, but I had commitment and drive and a willingness to do what was asked of me and what was required. A lot of that is to do with lifestyle and preparation. To me, that commitment was something I never really had to think about. I wanted to play for Dublin, I was picked to be here, so I'm going to be here. Yes, I would have to turn down lots of other things going on. I didn't have a summer holiday any of the years that I played. There were no music festivals, very few nights out. But that was my life and that was okay with me. I saw training sessions as my social outings. It was where my friends were and through the hard work we had great craic and when the time allowed we made up for our 'missed' nights out and had amazing times together. You are training or playing matches most days of the week so you get into whatever routine you have to. That's where your preparation comes in without even realising. If you are going straight to training then you make sure to have your food and drinks with you. You have all your gear ready to go. Sort out your work roster weeks in advance when you get your fixtures list. Lifestyle and preparation for me come hand in hand. And yes, it may not be the same lifestyle that your group of friends from school have, but to be honest you really don't look at it as a different lifestyle, because it's yours and that's what you want.

At times, it can be a challenging kind of lifestyle, but when you find that group of players who are all of the same mindset and are all giving the same commitment and the same passion to the team, then you get something special out of it. It's hard to explain, there's really nothing like it.

Aaron Kernan
ARMAGH FOOTBALLER 2004-2014

Kernan has enjoyed success with Armagh, winning four Ulster Championships, two National Leagues and an u21 All-Ireland title. He was named Young Footballer of the Year in 2005. He has also had great success with his club team, Crossmaglen Rangers. He joined the Cross senior team in 200. Since then he has won sixteen Armagh County medals, eight Ulster club medals and three All-Ireland club medals in 2007, 2011 and 2012. He won Man of the Match for his performance in the 2007 All-Ireland Club Final.

Nutrition

Following a healthy balanced diet is as important as any S&C programme. One will not function properly without the other. Putting dirty diesel into a car will affect its performance; putting the wrong food into our bodies has the exact same impact.

At the most basic level, nutrition is important for athletes because it provides a source of energy required to perform in our chosen sports. The food we eat impacts on our strength, training, performance and recovery.

I'm very fortunate that my wife is a dietician, which helps keep me on track with the meals and snacks we have at home. But there's none of us perfect and it's hard to stay on track 24/7, but sticking to a balanced diet 80 per cent of the time as well as exercising regularly will help us reach our potential.

Gym

S&C is a massive part of modern-day football. Regardless of the time of year, in or out of season I always try to maintain a decent level of conditioning. I understand my body well enough at this stage to know what works for me and what doesn't.

A good S&C programme should help enhance your flexibility and strength while most importantly helping to decrease your chances of picking up injuries. I've always stuck religiously to the programme and advice given to me at both club and county level from our S&C coaches.

Skill Development

The best advice I ever received was from my dad. As a young boy, I always remember him preaching to 'do the simple things well'.

By working on our basic skills, we make ourselves harder to mark. Being able to secure possession first time, pass to our teammate's advantage, kick and fist pass off either hand and foot might seem like the most obvious advice we could offer, but being able to execute them while under pressure is what separates the good from the great in our games.

Mindset

We all play sport for enjoyment, if we don't then what's the point? But having drive and purpose in your chosen sport is essential if you want to achieve your true potential.

There's ups and downs in sport, but having the self-belief to bounce back from these setbacks and not getting carried away by reaching your goals are key attributes that allow the best performers achieve success year after year.

Lifestyle

Maintaining a balanced lifestyle is vital. Having a job that you find rewarding and friends' company you enjoy socially are hugely important. Too many put their complete focus into their chosen sport, but for your own sanity it's important to have a release and enjoy the real world.

Match Preparation

My preparation would always follow a similar pattern. I'd be very particular with what I eat and the times I eat. I always make sure to have my kit bag ready in good time so there are no last-minute distractions.

Having everything in order allows me to make sure my focus is clear to concentrate on my performance.

Advice for your younger self

Whatever sport you choose, enjoy it. The social and physical benefits along with friendships to be gained from sports will last a lifetime.

Tony Óg Regan
GALWAY HURLER 2004-2013

An All-Ireland winner at minor, Regan was called up to Galway's intermediate team, winning an All-Ireland Intermediate Championship. The following year he was among the Tribesmen's senior ranks, winning two National Leagues and a Leinster Championship. The three-time all-star nominee has also worked as a performance psychologist with Tipperary from 2016-18, Galway hurling and football 2015-2019 and Limerick hurling team in 2019.

Dear younger self,

There is a great vehicle to express yourself through the experience of playing and being involved in sport. You will develop many great qualities through this experience that you may not fully realise now as a young person. The ability to communicate and relate to others will serve you well in any situation. The ability to commit to practising something and staying at it until it is a skill you are comfortable using under the highest pressure. The practice you do away from the sport on your own will make the game easier for you when the challenge is at its greatest. This belief that our talent is not fixed, we can learn and develop any skill with quality of focus and repetition, will spread across every aspect of our lives.

Embrace the challenges and knockbacks that life will inevitably bring and see them as learning moments and facing into growing as a person. Accept that WHAT YOU DO is not WHO YOU ARE. We will have many roles in life be it an athlete, friend, son, daughter, father, mother, manager, lawyer, doctor. The mind will want us at times to overvalue the importance of these roles. It is important to separate you the performer from who you really are. You mean many different things to many different people.

We can have wins and losses in sport and life, but they do not define who we are. People love you because of how you make them feel. Keep showing up with love, joy, peace and kindness for yourself, the community, and others in life. Great moments and memories can be created every day in many ways. Be open to new ideas, people, perspectives, and experiences. Enjoy the journey and stop overly worrying about the destination or outcome. Be fully present in the here and now. This is where inner joy, peace and confidence lives most of the time. Do the things that excite you, be around the people that make you feel good about yourself and the future, listen to and observe people that inspire you. Treat your mind well with positive and helpful thoughts, take care of yourself with good wholesome and nourishing foods. Move the body every day, spend time in nature, help others, clean up your environment and reflect on what went well today and what you are thankful for in life right now.

Enjoy the journey. Be honest, kind and caring. Bring laughter and playfulness to life.

Best wishes
Tony Óg Regan

Chrissy McKaigue
DERRY FOOTBALLER 2008-PRESENT

McKaigue has enjoyed a rake of success with his club Slaughtneil in both codes winning five Derry football titles, five Derry Hurling titles, two Ulster club hurling titles and three Ulster football club titles. McKaigue also represented Ireland in the 2013 International Rules Series. With Derry, he has won three National Leagues.

Nutrition

With so much advice available today on nutrition it's important not to get side-tracked by the new in-vogue diets. Find a template that works for you and stick consistently to it. Consistency in what you eat is the biggest thing regarding nutrition.

Strength and conditioning

It seems to be the phrase on everyone's lips nowadays. It's hugely important, but it's not about size or looks; it's about health. Getting stronger doesn't always equate to looks or hitting certain numbers in a one-off lift. S&C is about giving your body the best chance to play every minute of every game. It's about a long career with the minimum stress placed on your body. It's about a good quality of life after you have finished playing. That is why good technique, flexibility and stretching are the most important areas of S&C. It took me a while to understand that.

Skill Development

Developing skill is always about repetition. The best players can do the basic skills well under pressure and under fatigue. Today's modern game requires huge athleticism, but the top players can match that with high levels of skill. Few have high levels of skill innately. The majority work relentlessly at improving their skills and most importantly their decision making – the biggest part of today's game in my opinion.

Mindset

Controlling the mind has always been one of the biggest challenges in sport irrespective of the level. A mindset is improved by accepting what you can control and then doing everything in your power to control those variables. Do that and that builds confidence. It's vital to always be a competitor and to give it your all. It will take you past a lot of the more talented lazy opponents.

Lifestyle

The type of person you are off the field is usually a reflection of the person you are on it. Being an athlete takes commitment, but it also takes humility and the ability to realise the power you possess in your local area. Being a role model ties into conducting yourself correctly all the time. For me this means living the right kind of lifestyle.

Preparation

Mental and physical preparation is about consistently doing what gives you the best chance of playing at the top of your game. Only you can decide what works best for you. Once you find that recipe don't discount the discipline it takes to consistently carry out the template that works for you. It's hard work!

Advice to younger self

Prepare hard for the hard days. Doing this means that the hard days won't come around too often!

Ken McGrath
WATERFORD HURLER 1996-2011

McGrath was a stalwart of the Waterford team for over a decade. His versatility was a key strength of his game, winning All-Stars at half-back, midfield and half-forward. Now a Sunday game pundit, the Waterford legend has won six Waterford titles and a Munster club title with Mount Sion. During his time with the Déise, he won a National League, four Munster titles, and three All-Stars over a fifteen-year career.

When I played centre-forward for Waterford/Mount Sion I worked extremely hard on consistent striking on the run (at full pace) for points off my right and left sides. To master this on the days/nights off from collective training I would go up to the club's senior field with a handful of sliotars and just go for maybe four strikes at a time all from various distances and angles from goal. Every strike and run was at full pace and intensity, varying the shots: one off the back foot, next cutting in from the left, next on the turn with back to goal and so on. I only went for four because I wanted it to mimic a game and so every strike was done with a purpose. I would jog in, get the sliotars, get the breathing right, back out again and off I'd go, always trying to visualise getting away from my marker. At times I'd purposely drop the ball or fumble, then retrieve it, always at full speed so when you had time in a match the point nearly felt easy.

I played centre forward all my life for the club so I did this throughout my career even when I was centre back for the county, as then the target was an area of the field where I needed to put the ball into the right corner, just beyond the half forward. Most of my striking was on the move and for the most part never really let me down. For me, the best modern players that are the best strikers of the ball are: Canning, TJ Reid, Callanan, Horgan, so for me it was always one of the most important skills to work on even if we can take it for granted at times.

Ger Brennan
DUBLIN FOOTBALLER 2006-2015

A hardy defender that wasn't afraid to play on the edge, perhaps Brennan's absence was noticed most in Dublin's 2014 All-Ireland semi-final defeat to Donegal. During his time with the Boys in Blue he won a National League, five Leinster titles and two All-Irelands. He has also won five Dublin SFC, four Leinster club titles and two All-Ireland Club Championships with his club, St Vincent's. He is currently a selector with the Carlow footballers.

What was your pre-match routine, and did you have any superstitions or rituals?

If the match was on a Sunday, I would spend most of the week focusing in on the opposition and looking at the individual player I was going to be marking, looking at their forward unit as a whole, how they move and interact with one another. It would always start with management and coaches; they would work hard in providing the resources and giving us a guide to the type of opponent you were facing. There was a level of responsibility given from coaches to players to go away and do the extra work because ultimately, it's the players who are on the pitch, not the coach. From there, you come up with your own strategies of marking that individual and as a defensive unit, your own defensive strategies to curb or lessen the impact of the forwards and how they impose themselves on the game. There's no value in the coach knowing how the opposition are going to set up, if the individual player hasn't done the work.

Over the years with Dublin, I was less superstitious the more experience I gained. I became more focused on the routine and repetition of the day and the morning in the build up to games. For me, it used to involve getting up at around 7:30-8, if it was a 4pm throw-in in Croke Park. I'd get up, get a good breakfast in, watch a bit of TV, head over to 10 o'clock mass, and go for a good 30-40-minute walk and a bit of stretching.

Then meet the team three hours beforehand for the pre-match meal. When I first started out under Pillar Caffrey we used to meet at DCU, later under Pat Gilroy and then Jim Gavin we'd meet at the Gibson Hotel. Pre-match routine there with the lads, maybe a couple of board games to pass the time and keep things relaxed. Before we leave for Croke Park, we'd have a 5-10-minute team meeting just to recap on the focus areas for each player and then onto the bus.

It's about finding the routine that suits you, which can take a bit of time to figure out over a couple of games/couple of years. If lads played well, sometimes they would do the exact same thing for the next match. Keep it simple, that's what worked for me.

How do you play on the edge without going over it?

It's probably something that players are born with or develop in their upbringing. In the early parts of my career, I would have gone over it on occasion, which would have resulted in the team being down to fourteen men. The learning from that is that ultimately all you are doing is a disservice to your teammates and putting them under pressure. The message I got from management was that if I continued to cross that line, they wouldn't be able to pick me because I'd be too much of a liability. It's trying to manage and curb that aggression and channel it into the right thing on the pitch. It's trying to be careful that you don't go overboard on the physical contact, though Gaelic games, Gaelic football and hurling, *are* very physical. To keep pushing things as a defender to the limit with a view to getting away with what you can get away with, without doing anything cowardly, but just pushing things to the boundary. Trying to put the forward off their game as best as you can, that's the way I see it.

What did you do after games?

Probably after a game I'd go and celebrate with the team and family, depending on how close we were to the next match. Most lads did and do enjoy that after a game. You would always very quickly move on to your next opponent and try to get the body right. We would have had a recovery session on the Monday evening, active recovery, and a very light jog with a bit of stretching, then jump into the sea or the pool, nothing overly exertive on the body. Active recovery is something that is key.

Self-Reflection

While it's important that you look at the opposition, it's more important to look at how you as a player can improve game to game, whether it's your ability to read the game, execute the basic skills or communication. A player should look to get feedback, good, bad or indifferent from management and coaches. Take it on board and look to apply it to training during the week, to try to get better. It's all about continuous improvement.

Gavin White
KERRY FOOTBALLER 2018-PRESENT

Following a successful minor career, winning two All-Irelands back to back in 2014 and 2015, it was expected that White would someday play for the Kingdom's seniors. Following a run of success with his club, Dr Crokes, which led to an All-Ireland club title, White was given his championship debut and a run of form saw him earn an all-star nomination. He has also won a National League and two Munster titles.

The best advice I can give? Concentrate on your skills. That's a major one. As you get older you will find that gym work begins to become a major part of your training regime, but don't worry too much about it. All you need to do is build a strong foundation for yourself in terms of technique and flexibility, so that you can use the gym properly when you're older. There's no need to be lifting big weights or anything like that as a young player, you have plenty of time to be doing that sort of stuff later. At the end of the day, we all want to be footballers not bodybuilders. For me, footballing skills is the main one. 'Bigger' players often seem to dominate in the younger age groups, but the players with a high skillset will always prevail.

Look at areas in your game that can be improved. Can you solo with both feet? Can you hand pass on either side? Can you kick a point off either leg? Perfecting these skills at a younger age will greater enhance your potential as you get older. It's so much easier to perfect these skills when you are younger. Even just having a ball in your hands every day will improve you as a football player. Smaller players may find it difficult at a young age, but trust that you have all the skills in the game and back yourself in everything you do. Don't worry if you're the smallest player on the pitch (I know what it feels like!). Keep working on the skills of the game and most importantly enjoy yourself, everything else will fall into place.

Mark Foley
LIMERICK HURLER 1995-2009

A two-time All-Star, Foley has made more appearances for the Treaty County than any other player. During his time with Limerick he won a National League and a

Munster title and was named Young Hurler of the Year in 1996. The former captain has also won five Limerick SHC with Adare.

Skills

No matter what way our ever-changing game evolves, it comes down to skill. At the minute it is a power game, where the physical attributes of strength, conditioning and speed are huge. It's still important not to forget that the basics never change and to really focus on the fundamentals all the time, especially on your own away from collective training. Work on control, first touch, catching and striking. Being able to hit off both sides, on the run left and right, going backwards left and right, over the shoulder if you can especially for forwards. First touch is probably the difference between a very good and excellent hurler, being able to control it while moving at full speed without breaking stride is huge. Being able to kill the ball and get it into your hand with one touch is massive. Handling has become a huge part of the game over the last number of years, keep working on high fielding. Being able to strike the ball straight to your hand without dropping or fumbling it no matter how hard it's coming at you. You can never practise these enough, they're the fundamentals the game is based on, no matter what way it evolves.

Nutrition and Lifestyle

I'm no nutritionist so I wouldn't be one to give expert advice, but from my own point of view, the best diet you can have is a balanced diet. Don't skip meals. Fuel before training and replace the calories that are burnt by eating after training.

Gym

I think it's very important when you're starting out on your S&C journey that you get the correct advice in terms of technique, that when you're lifting weights that you're sure you're doing it correctly. I know lots of the guys playing with Limerick at the moment started that in the academy. When you start adding weights and start gradually strengthening up, make sure that your technique is strong, that you're working the right areas and that you're not going to do any damage to yourself.

Advice to my Younger Self

Just make sure you enjoy it. We play the games because we want to enjoy them. Winning is great, improving is great. Respect your coaches, they're doing their best to try and help you. Make loads of friends along the way, don't forget everyone is trying to work together to make your team better and improve you individually. Don't take it too seriously, enjoy the journey, it will give you years and years of enjoyment. We all want to win, we all want to be successful, but really enjoy it and the friendships you make along the way.

Philip Jordan
TYRONE FOOTBALLER 2002-2011

A mainstay of the Tyrone team of the 2000s, Jordan played with the perfect balance of attack and defence, winning two National Leagues, four Ulster titles, three All-Irelands and four All-Stars (the most of any Tyrone defender). Following his retirement, he has been remembered as one of Tyrone's greatest players.

The most important thing for any player is to remember why they are playing the game. You must enjoy the sport, otherwise what is the point in giving the time to train and play matches? Once you get to senior level things become much more serious and now is the time to enjoy playing it.

When you are young you don't have the time demands of work. Make sure to use that time to work on the skills of the game. I was constantly kicking the ball against the wall and roof of our house at home. Kicking off both feet, hand passing, catching and handling skills must be mastered and you need to constantly work on these to make sure you make the best of your ability.

I always had a pretty simple outlook. I would aim for perfection, but accept that achieving perfection is never possible. However, aiming for the perfect game allowed me to push myself to constantly improve. I believe that helped me to achieve my dream of playing for Tyrone. Whilst there were more talented players, I was always looking at ways to improve my game and my attitude towards a setback was to work harder. Hard work means you can realise your potential and that is all anyone can expect of you.

Don't be afraid to play other sports. There will always come a time when decisions will have to be made about which sport you want to focus on, but during your school years is not that time. I played basketball in school until I was sixteen and I've no doubt many of the skills developed on the court helped my game out on the football pitch.

Your dream may be to play the game with your friends at any level, it may be to play for your club and for some it will be to play for the county. Regardless of what your dream is, don't let anyone tell you that you cannot achieve it. Dreams are what motivate us all to achieve our best.

Chloe Sigerson
CORK CAMOGIE PLAYER 2017-PRESENT

Sigerson first played for the Rebelettes at intermediate level in 2016 and was a key part of the Leesiders' run to the All-Ireland final, winning a Soaring Star Award at the end of the year. A call-up to the senior squad was inevitable. An attacking asset from halfback, the two-time All-Star Killeagh defender specialises in long-range shooting and free taking. She has won back-to-back All-Irelands in 2017 and 2018 and was nominated for POTY in 2018.

The gym is becoming more important to the life of an inter-county female player. Each year the game of camogie evolves, and the player must adapt. The year 2020 was the trialling of new playing rules which included increased physicality. This meant as players we had to be able to withstand a harder tackle. My advice would be to keep it simple, the gym does not have to be a two-hour session every day. You can get what you need in forty minutes three times a week.

Nutrition in GAA to me is the most important thing. Our bodies are constantly being put under stress from pitch and gym sessions, so we must fuel our bodies accordingly and recover correctly in a way that we can perform again the next day. People always ask, am I on a strict diet? My answer is NO, it is not a diet. It's become a habit for me to make the right choices 90 per cent of the time, and this allows me to enjoy my food.

I am a student in college, so my life revolves around training and study. My preparation for a day in college followed by training that evening is very important. I need to have my gear ready, in the car, and meals prepped the day before. This day could involve leaving the house at 7am and not coming home until 9/10pm so organisation is key. Always be prepared as this allows your day to run smoothly with little stress.

The standard of skills in GAA are raised each year. The basics remain the same, but the touch is quicker and sharper. For me it is important to keep these skills to a high standard. A simple wall at the side of your house can keep you on top of this. The spectacular skills of sideline cuts and flicks are what comes with practice and confidence. A player who has won the last three balls in a game is more likely to have the confidence to try a flick or a rarely seen skill than the player who has missed the last three balls and is now playing on edge and doubting their capabilities. I'd advise my younger self to enjoy every win that comes along. The rate at which teams are improving these days means the wins don't come around as often. Also enjoy life outside of GAA. Plenty of players, especially inter-county, miss opportunities to go on summer holidays or events so take the chances when they come along. Life is for living at the end of the day.

Kevin Cassidy
DONEGAL FOOTBALLER 2002-2011

If you look up 'Kevin Cassidy' on YouTube, one the first videos is of his winning point against Kildare in the 2011 All-Ireland quarter-final. What's missing from the clip is the wide he kicked from nearly the same position moments earlier. This showed the composure and self-belief he brought to his game anytime he took to the field, winning three Donegal club titles, an Ulster club title, a National League, an Ulster title and two All-Stars along the way.

My advice to any young person growing up nowadays would be to try your hand at as many sports as possible if you are sport minded. All sports have some sort of crossover so by playing different ones you will strengthen other parts of your game in your preferred sport. Growing up I played a lot of soccer, GAA, basketball and some tennis and I believe you can gain so much from the movements and skills of other sports. Come the age of sixteen or seventeen you will probably have to focus on one particular sport and put all your efforts into that sport if you hope to reach the top. When you make that decision my advice to you would be to be totally committed to it. Train hard and train smart, always research for ways to help you improve yourself.

Every coach or manager will teach you something. You may not agree with them, but trust me you will still pick up at least one thing off each that will make you a better athlete. We never stop learning. Even today I am still learning. Stay humble, stay hungry and no matter what, never neglect your education or profession because when that final whistle blows on whatever sport you play you still have to earn an income and provide for yourself and your family.

Ádh Mór

Rena Buckley

Noel McGrath

Colm Galvin

Derek Lyng

THE MIDFIELDERS' ADVICE

Gary Brennan

Sarah Rowe

Noel McGrath

TIPPERARY HURLER 2009-PRESENT

With a highly successful underage career, winning a Munster Minor title, two Minor All-Irelands, two u21 Munster Titles and an u21 All-Ireland, McGrath managed to break into Tipperary's starting fifteen at just eighteen. Since then McGrath has proven to be one of the top hurlers in the country, claiming four Munster titles, three All-Irelands, three All-Stars, Young Hurler of the Year 2009 and MOTM in All-Ireland final 2019. A dual player with his club Loughmore-Castleiney, he's won three Tipperary SFC, two Tipperary SHC and a Munster Club Hurling Championship.

For any young person looking to play sport at a high level it's important to have the commitment and interest in your sport. If you have these then you will enjoy it much more. Enjoyment is the main reason I play sport.

During the teenage years, there are many other challenges that young people face. It's important to make the right choices during this time as it will benefit you both on and off the field. Listen to people you know and trust, such as parents and coaches, as they will be doing their best to steer you in the right direction in your daily life and also in your sporting life.

When it comes to the game, I would advise everyone to practise as much as possible and to pay attention to coaches at training. You will never know it all! Practice away from training is also a good idea and this can be in the form of meeting friends to play a fun game of your choice or on your own with a hurley and ball or football against the wall at home.

And always respect your teammates, opponents, coaches and parents.

Gary Brennan

CLARE FOOTBALLER 2007-2021

The former Clare captain had the perfect balance to his game; he paired his ability as one of the best high fielders in the country with being a classy footballer. The

2016 All-Star nominee has also proven to be a strong hurler, winning two Clare County Championships along with a Munster title. The Ballyea man has also represented Ireland in two International Rules Series in 2015 and 2017.

'What makes a brilliant player? What do you need to do to become an inter-county player? What is the secret?'

These are questions that I often asked myself as a teenager, questions that I longed to have answered. I looked for some magic recipe that I could copy and use for myself. Perhaps there is some trick that I haven't discovered, but my experience of being an inter-county player for the last thirteen years has taught me that it is unlikely to be the case. The reality is that a series of good habits will help you to become a better person, and in turn a better player. What are those habits?

• Try to improve yourself at every opportunity – skills, physical condition, lifestyle, mental preparation.

• Learn from those around you and be open to feedback and willing to work on your weaknesses – where you are now doesn't have to be where you stay. I never made any county development squads at u14, u15, u16, and u17, but ended up as captain at u18.

• Set yourself little goals that you can control and work towards them. When you achieve them, reward yourself and target your next improvement.

• Believe in yourself – it sounds very simple, but comes from knowing you're working hard. I have always said that I believe the difference between the very best players and the rest of us is the ability to perform the skills of the game at pace and under pressure. I am a big believer in strength and conditioning and mental preparation, but without the skills of the game, their impact is limited. Make the development of your skills your number one priority. All you need is a ball and a wall to begin with. You can increase the challenge over time.

In short, try to be the very best you can be, and you can do no more.

Remember, you can be better than you even realise. The only limits are those you set for yourself. But if you do happen to come across that magic secret, be sure to let me know!

Paddy Keenan
LOUTH FOOTBALLER 2003-2014

The only Louth player to ever win an All-Star, Keenan was a pivotal figure at midfield for the Wee County during his twelve-year career. He won two National Leagues, an All-Star in 2010 and represented Ireland in the International Rules series the same year. The former Louth captain has also won seven Louth SFC with St Patricks GFC.

Gym

In my younger days, I was fairly focused on lifting heavy weights and bulking up, largely because I was relatively small for a midfielder at county level. However, after suffering from some fairly debilitating injuries, I began to learn a lot more about my body and what I needed to do to keep it in prime condition for football. I then put more value on flexibility, core strength, body movement and injury prevention. In my later years, I definitely wasn't as big or strong in the traditional sense, but I felt much better and found I was experiencing fewer injuries and able to recover far quicker after games.

Nutrition

I am obsessed with food so I was (and still am) able to keep my diet and nutrition at a fairly high level. I think it's extremely important to have access to a quality nutritionist with a background in sports. There are so many so-called 'experts' in the nutrition field these days; social media can be a problem in that unqualified people can publish misleading or incorrect advice and promote fad diets that may do more harm than good in the long term. While I can now be a little looser with my diet, I generally keep it simple: loads of fruit and veg and good quality proteins, limit the sugar intake and avoid processed foods where possible. Consistently hydrating throughout the day can't be underestimated.

Lifestyle

Generally, I'd live a pretty quiet life as my wife and I aren't big party animals. However, I really believe that for young sportspeople, it is hugely important to find a balance away from their sport. It's very easy to neglect your education, family and other hobbies when you're so focused on your sporting career. Don't be too hard on yourself and don't feel guilty for taking a day off to unwind or for having a bit of junk food. Everything in moderation once you get the basics right.

Preparation

I was always very particular about my preparation, whether it was training, games or even the gym. Having a routine, particularly on game days, is important as it allows you to focus on the game rather than stressing about your food, gear etc. Simple things like making a list of your gear or packing your bag the night before always helped me.

Skill Practice

These days, it's very easy to commit a lot of time to the gym rather than focusing on the basic skills of your sport. To me, your gym work should complement your skills, not the other way around. Getting to training twenty to thirty minutes earlier was always important to me as it gave me a window where I could practise free kicks/shooting etc before the rest of the team arrived. I pretty much always had a ball in my hand, mainly to practise my weaker side: soloing, pick-ups, fist passing off a wall, kicking; I just continually practised the basics until my weaker side was nearly as good as my strong side. A two-footed player is a much more difficult one to stop in game situations.

Advice to younger self

The main one would be to stretch more and do more yoga! I experienced a few bad injuries in my playing days, some of which I still suffer from now. Unfortunately, I probably didn't have the knowledge or awareness of the impact my training and playing had on my body and I just tried to play through everything. Taking the time to improve your mobility and flexibility will help you extend your career and avoid injuries over the longer term.

Shane McGrath
TIPPERARY HURLER 2006-2015

The Tipp team's driving force for over a decade, McGrath showed time and time again why he was a fan-favourite. While in college he won two Fitzgibbons with Limerick IT. The two-time All-Star always wore his heart on his sleeve, winning a National League, being named Munster POTY in 2008, five Munster titles and an All-Ireland in 2010.

Advice to young players

When you are young play every sport you're interested in. Each sport will help you learn a skill or discipline that you can use to help you succeed in the sport you love the most. By sixteen or seventeen you will know which sport you have the most passion for.

If you really want to make it to the top level, then you must be willing to miss out on things that your friends are doing. You can have success or excuses in life, but you can't have both. If hurling is your passion, then doing this should be a privilege not a pain.

What you do on your own away from training will separate the good from the top-class players. If you have a concern about your game, work on that until it becomes your strength. As the saying goes, 'The more I practise, the luckier I get!'

And finally enjoy the journey ... if you can't enjoy yourself then what you're doing is not for you.

Believe in yourself ... even if nobody else does.

John O'Loughlin
LAOIS FOOTBALLER 2008-PRESENT

A Leinster medallist at both minor and u21 levels, O'Loughlin has been a key player for Laois. In his time with the O'Moore County he has won a National League, represented Ireland in the 2015 International Rules Series and won a Dublin SFC with St. Brigid's.

Gym

Strength and conditioning are important aspects of Gaelic games performance. The physicality of Gaelic football means that players, especially young athletes, must be structurally strong and conditioned to compete safely. Playing inter-county football, I try to incorporate at least two gym sessions a week throughout the season. Whether it's a collective gym session or individual session it is imperative to get these sessions done consistently throughout the season. The main reasons I go to the gym are to increase muscle mass, to become more explosive on the pitch, and to prevent injury. Muscle mass is important in Gaelic football because you have to be strong enough to hold off opponents. Being explosive is important because you have to be able to break tackles, and injury prevention speaks for itself – nobody likes being injured and missing matches! Inter-county teams are quite lucky as they generally have S&C coaches of great expertise. They give us programmes that are individually tailored to the specific individual.

Nutrition

I take my nutrition very seriously and am always trying to further my knowledge on exactly what I should be eating and when I should be eating to optimise my performance on the pitch. Good nutrition helps me recover quicker after training, games and gym sessions. I do a weekly shop every Sunday and get all the food that I will need for the week ahead. I make sure to include plenty of the three macronutrients in my diet – fat, carbohydrate and protein. The ultimate goal of my nutrition plan is to ensure I achieve optimal energy output at the times of training/matches and recover from both. I eat a lot of oily fish, salmon, for example, for the good fats, and omega three. I eat a lot of leafy vegetables like kale, spinach and broccoli. I also eat a lot of potatoes, primarily sweet potatoes, for a steady energy source.

Lifestyle

The most important thing for me as a Gaelic footballer is to live a balanced lifestyle. I do this by making sure I have other important things in my life as well as football. My job as a primary-school teacher is something I enjoy and get great job satisfaction out of. Relationships with family, friends, staff and team members is important also. I have a keen interest in reading books, and I find this is a great way to relax and educate myself at the same time. As I already mentioned nutrition is important to me, but it is important to strike a balance in that as well, and that all comes under the remit of a balanced lifestyle.

Preparation

Preparation for me starts when I do my grocery shopping every Sunday. Preparing for the week ahead, whether the training load is going to be light or heavy it is my job to be prepared for that with regard to what I eat and with regard to my own personal recovery. When I have a match coming up at the weekend it is my job to be as best prepared as I can for that match, who am I playing against, who will I be marking, what are his strengths and how do I attack his weaknesses. It is also very important to have my laundry done and my correct gear for training and matches.

Skill Practice

To me this is the single most important aspect of being a Gaelic footballer. Gym and nutrition are great additives to help me perform to the best of my ability, but they are not replacements for the most significant aspect of being a Gaelic footballer and that is being good at the basic skills of the game. The basic skills include being able to solo, and kick with both feet, hand pass with both hands, catch the ball over my head, catch the ball at the earliest possible time that it can be caught. I practise these skills once a week for sixty minutes outside of training. I have ten of my own O'Neill's footballs, so I never have an excuse not to practise. After every training I stay out on the pitch for an extra twenty minutes to practise these skills as well as practising catching the ball from the goalkeeper's kickouts. Any time I am going training or practising my skills on my own, I aim to leave the field with 1,000 ball contacts.

Advice to my younger self

Don't be afraid to make mistakes. Be a bit kinder and more compassionate to yourself. Don't take defeats so personally. Don't believe everything you think, thoughts are just that – thoughts. Football is important, but there is more to life than football and sport. Be the best all-round person you can be and then football and sport will take care of itself.

Colm Galvin
CLARE HURLER 2012-PRESENT

During a hugely successful underage career, Galvin won two Munster minor championships. Three u21 Munster Championships and three All-Ireland u21 Championships. While in college he won two Fitzgibbons with Mary I. The 2013 All-Ireland winner has also won individual awards including two u21 All-Stars, the 2014 U21 Player of the year and an All-Star.

The main piece of advice I could give to any young person is to enjoy the game. If you're not having a laugh or a smile on your face, it's not enjoyable. Of course there are serious moments, but when I look back it seems like anytime I went out training, I was laughing. Most of all it was to get to see my friends on the team. Some of us were in different secondary schools and at training I got to see them and have the craic.

In February/March 2020, I had a groin injury. Basically, the bones were hitting off each other, it felt like it was burning anytime I was running. It would come and go every few days, and when I'd try to play a game, I would have to come off or not start. I went to the Sports Clinic in Santry, they were unbelievable. My recovery was a lot of movement-based work with a resistance band. It's a slow process, but the goal is to get back fully fit. At times it feels like a disaster, because it's so slow and time consuming. Running pain free is the goal that Santry gave me and that's what I'm working towards.

Fiona McHale
MAYO FOOTBALLER 2004-PRESENT

The engine of the Mayo team for more than a decade, McHale has been a crucial figure both on the pitch and in the dressing room. The 2016 All-Star has won four Connacht Championships and three O'Connor cups with DCU and two with UL.

With her club Carnacon, she's won twenty Mayo Club championships, fourteen-Connacht Club Championships and six All-Ireland Club championships.

Whatever you do always give your best. Play and train as if it's your last! Take advice from your coaches and work on this feedback. Ask your coaches what areas you can improve on. Always look to get better. Encourage your teammates to do their best also. Don't underestimate the power of your encouragement to your teammates.

Practise your skills outside of training time, particularly your non-dominant side. Practise at your local pitch or against a wall at home. If you don't have a football buy one. If you don't have the opportunity to buy one, borrow one from your club. Take a bag of balls from your coach and practise your shooting on days when you don't have training. Bring a friend!

Stick to the game. Sport has given me so many opportunities and many great times in my life. The majority of these experiences have been so good because of the friends that I have made along the way. We cannot enjoy every single minute of training or games. There will be rocky patches along the way, but no matter what, stay playing the game because it will give you many rewards in life.

Kevin Feely
KILDARE FOOTBALLER 2016-PRESENT

Without doubt one of the finest midfielders in the country, Feely is a springboard for Kildare's attack through midfield. A Kildare SFC winner with Athy, he represented Ireland in the 2017 International Rules Series. The 2017 All-Star nominee is also a skilful soccer player, having played at clubs such as Bohemians, Charlton Athletic and AFC Wimbledon.

Skill Development

The most important aspect of football and hurling is your skill level and how consistent you are under pressure with your skill execution. As a young player there is no end to the amount of practice you can do under various conditions to improve your skill level. My favourite thing to practise as a young player was to try and be equally good off either foot and either hand when it came to kicking, hand passing, soloing and even catching with one hand or the other. This usually meant a lot of time spent on my own in the garden or the GAA pitch trying to repeat what I had seen on the television by my favourite players (Michael Donnellan, Padraic Joyce, Dermot Earley, Declan O'Sullivan, and Johnny Doyle). So if they happened to be left footed I would try and do everything they did left footed and the same thing for the right footers. The most important thing about it was that I spent a huge amount of time practising and was able to imagine and visualise very easily every situation that could happen in a match while I was practising. This stood to me a huge amount when it came to matches and made practising never seem like hard work.

Strength Work

As a young player I was quite small and also very skinny so I found that strength, power and speed were things that didn't come naturally to me. Often I was able to rely on quick thinking and skills to get me out of trouble, but as I got older I realised that I would have to work hard on getting stronger or I would fall behind. My advice to players in the twelve to fifteen years old age group would be start trying bodyweight exercises to develop good control and good core strength.

As a teenager I invested in a pull-up bar to put in my room doorframe and started out with simple upper body exercises like push-ups and pull-ups. I would do as many reps as I could (this was a very small amount to begin with!) then take a two-minute rest and then do as many as I could again. I would repeat this for three or four sets and usually do it three or four times a week. For core strength I learned from a workshop that

Peter Canavan gave that the plank and side plank exercises were excellent for giving you the ability to take and give hits well and keep a low centre of gravity when trying to get out of tackles. I would aim to hold the plank position for sixty to ninety seconds and repeat it three times. For the side plank exercise I would aim for thirty to forty-five seconds on each side and repeat three times as well. For strengthening my legs I used some light dumbbells to do squats, overhead squats and lunges. Usually I would do three sets of ten-twelve repetitions of these exercises. This will help to develop speed and power for jumping to catch high balls especially.

Rena Buckley
CORK DUAL PLAYER 2003-2018

The first player to captain Cork to both All-Ireland senior championships. Buckley is without a doubt one of the most successful players of all time, winning three Camogie National Leagues, seven Camogie All-Irelands, eleven Football National Leagues, eleven Football All-Irelands, six Football All-Stars and five Camogie All-Stars. She also won two Ashbourne Cups with UCD and three All-Ireland club titles with Donoughmore.

Having a balanced lifestyle is very important for everyone. Without a balanced life, I don't think being content with life over a long period is possible. And being content, whether we are an athlete or not, is what we are all looking for at the end of the day. An athlete can only really play at the top of his or her game consistently if he or she is content.

Being physically healthy and ready to perform in sport is key to success. We all know that. We know we must prepare our bodies for the task at hand through appropriate training. We know that if we get injured, we must rehabilitate the injury. We know we must eat well in order for our body to work as well as it can and to have the energy we crave to perform.

Sometimes as athletes, we can forget about the other bits and pieces that make up the jigsaw. We can forget about how important being mentally and emotionally healthy is for performance. Having a laugh or a big catch up with family or friends can be as important as training. Having time just to be, without distraction, is important for the mind to relax and to figure out the things that we haven't time to dwell on in our busy existence. Being grateful for all the people who support us. Getting the chance to give someone support is rewarding. Being organised and on top of your work helps reduce unwanted work/study stress. And of course, sleep is one of the most important parts of all of our days. It's when the body rests and recovers and when the mind processes.

My advice to my younger self would be to look at your whole life and make sure that there's balance there, most of the time. Sometimes something unexpected crops up, and that's OK too. But in general, to make sure I'm enjoying life by working/studying well, training well, eating and sleeping well, keeping up the important relationships with family and friends, taking some 'me time' and being grateful for all the good things in our lives. I reckon that's about as well as anyone can do. The tricky bit is to figure out the balance between them all!

Conor Ryan
CLARE HURLER 2013-2016

Following success at u21 level winning a Munster and All-Ireland Championship, Ryan was drafted into the Banner's senior team. His performances during his break-out season saw him win many accolades including MOTM in the drawn final, an All-Ireland and an All-Star. A dual player with his club, Cratloe, he's also won two Clare SFC and two Clare SHC.

There are so many demands on the modern-day GAA player in order to perform at the top level and sometimes it can seem like a mountain to climb, but one thing I always used as a point of reference was to 'control the controllables' and let the rest take care of itself. I remember my six-year-old self asking Brian Lohan in 1997 when he brought the Liam McCarthy cup to our primary school if he ever got nervous before matches. His response was, 'No never, if I have prepared as best I can then there's no more to be done, if something goes wrong after that then so be it'.

From my own experiences and taking a retrospective look at the few times I was lucky enough to be able to kick and puck a ball for my club and county, there are things that I would certainly have focused on more. Firstly, I now realise the importance of setting goals. A goal is never a plan unless it is written down and tracked. Sure, we all want to win county and All-Ireland titles and they can sound like lofty goals. But break it down into small parts.

What I would say to any young player is to set your goals for your field, gym sessions and nutrition around weekly targets; what you want to work on and improve in a given week. After every training and gym session, I ask myself, 'Have I improved a skill or technique, have I made myself better at one aspect of my game by showing up here today?' Set milestones at drills; the number of touches, shots, hooks, blocks. Track these numbers and try and improve each week. Putting metrics on targets makes it easier to track progress, like you would in a gym keeping track of those rising bench-press numbers. Having these short, achievable milestones allows you to maintain focus and you will see big differences week in, week out. Look at these goals in the context of the 'why'. What is it that drives you towards being the best you can be, because when you know the 'why', the 'how' becomes a more enjoyable and worthwhile journey.

Rather than over-commit and become obsessed, balance is vitally important in today's game. While there is a lot that goes into playing at a high level, it is important to enjoy every minute of it; that team environment is the thing you will miss the most when you hang up the boots. Because of the level of commitment and sacrifice required now of players, if it's not enjoyable then it's not worthwhile. Life is about balance and GAA is just a part of our lives, an incredible part, but it is important to enjoy it, focus the time on becoming the best you can be, but leave enough time to enjoy the simple things in life. I think one huge lesson we can all take from the covid19 pandemic, is that there is a world outside GAA. Happy players make better players and better people.

Sarah Rowe
MAYO FOOTBALLER 2012-PRESENT

An all-round athlete, Rowe has excelled in whichever sport she has tried her hand at, be it football, soccer or Aussie Rules. In soccer she has won an FAI women's Cup, a Women's National League, a WNL cup, a WFAI intermediate cup and also represented Ireland at underage and senior level. In Football she has won an O'Connor Cup with DCU. Her performances with Mayo got her noticed by Collingwood who she now plays for in the AFLW where she won Multicultural POTY in her first season.

Advice to my younger self

For me it's all about hard work. You gain a lot of confidence from working hard, because the one person in your life you can't fool is yourself. When you know you've done the work you can bring that confidence into games.

You have to be able to listen to the people around you and be able to take feedback. Nine times out of ten if someone's giving you feedback it's to try to make you a better player. Coaches can see things in your game that maybe you can't see yourself.

Keep an open mind. Get better, try new things. In terms of S&C and running, I think it's really important that instead of thinking you know it all, listen to experts in their fields.

The benefit of playing multiple sports

Playing multiple sports has definitely given me a stronger character. I've had to be resilient. Playing soccer with Ireland I'd a few tough years where I wasn't getting selected, then selected, dropped and selected again. Times like that really test you, because you're used to being in an environment like your club or somewhere where you're constantly excelling. It's the times you get knocked back that teach you the most about yourself and your character. You can hide by blaming other people, but it needs to come from within. Reflect on yourself and your ability and what you can do better. Control the controllables.

I think being involved in a lot of different team environments like soccer, football and AFL have taught me how important it is to have a strong team culture. You can't get anywhere without your teammates. What works for me mightn't work for you, but it's important that we all work together. It's about finding a way to work with other players, who don't think the same way as you. Remember your way is not the only way.

How different is the professional environment of the AFL to the GAA?

I'm very grateful that I have the opportunity to play both. I absolutely love playing for Mayo. Pride of place, pride of community, for your family and your friends and all the reasons we do it are amazing. It's a lot of hard work with travel but it's always worth it and when you win big games it's really worth it.

When it comes to the AFL it's a completely different way of thinking. It's essentially a business and run like one. You get treated very well because you have all the facilities around you. The GAA and AFL are completely different, obviously amateur vs professional. While similar with similar mindsets you don't watch soccer and football and try to compare them because they're completely different.

Sport is such an important part of my life, it's given me everything. My life does revolve around it, but I have created good habits for myself so that I can switch off and enjoy other parts of my life and long may it continue.

Jarlath Óg Burns
ARMAGH FOOTBALLER 2019-PRESENT

Son of the Armagh legend Jarlath Burns, you could say that high-fielding is in Burns' genes. The 2019 All-Star nominee has added a platform from midfield that the Orchard County lacked in previous seasons.

Preparation

It's important to get the correct amount of sleep before and after training or matches. It doesn't seem like a big thing, but it is. As well as that, stretching and foam rolling before your training is vital. It ensures that your body is ready for intense activity.

Mindset

It's crucial that you believe in your own ability, which comes with practice. You have to be confident on the field or you won't stand out from the crowd. If you go through the motions and don't try new things that you have practised on your own, what's the point?

Advice to my younger self

Drop all other sports! Pick one and get very good at it because that will take time and you don't have time to try and play others just for a bit of craic.

Derek Lyng
KILKENNY HURLER 2001-2010

A true warrior who played with a blend of commitment, work rate and skill. Before linking up with the senior team, Lyng won a raft of honours including a Fitzgibbon with Waterford IT, Leinster and All-Ireland u21 Championships and a Leinster Intermediate Championship. The two-time All-Star won four National Leagues, nine Leinster titles, and six All-Irelands. He has also won a Kilkenny JHC with Emeralds. The former Kilkenny selector is now the Cats' u20s manager.

Gym

Being able to compete physically with your opponents has become hugely important in the modern game. Regardless of shape or size you can improve your strength and power over time. It is vital to follow a qualified S&C coach's plan so you are following a tailored programme for your own needs. It is important to not jump ahead in trying to lift heavy weights and to make sure you can do all the movements correctly and with good form before adding weight to any exercise.

Nutrition

As you get older the part nutrition plays in your preparation increases, most especially when you are training. It is about knowing the choices you have when deciding what to eat, especially when snacking. The watchouts are trying to steer away from sugary drinks and snacks. It's important to eat a well-balanced diet to help with growth and provide you with enough energy to train well.

Lifestyle

This is about balance. While you can be focused on improving your game in hurling or football, you also need time to enjoy other hobbies, interests, studies and friends to make sure you continue to develop all aspects of your life. Of course, be ambitious and know what you want and work hard to improve, but also keep in mind there is a life outside of that as well.

Preparation

Best advice I was given when preparing for big games was to embrace the nerves. Being nervous before any challenge is inevitable. The key is to not waste your time or energy worrying about being too nervous, trying to hide or run away from it. It is better if you can learn to recognise it and then use it to drive you once you hit the pitch on the day of a game.

Skill Enhancement

The fact remains that the more time you have a hurl and ball in your hand the better hurler you will become. Striking, controlling and subtly changing the grip on your hurl will allow you to perform these skills when it matters. My advice is simple but effective – get outside and practise, all you need is your hurl, ball and a wall (mind the windows!).

Advice to My Younger Self

If I could go back and have a word in the ear of my younger self, I would say two things:

1) Just aim to get the most out of yourself. Comparing yourself to others for better or worse is futile. Your goal should be to develop yourself and challenge yourself to your own limits. Your sporting (and life!) journey is your own and you have the ultimate control.

2) Don't attach your success to outcomes or results. Wins and losses – winners' medals or being dropped off panels – will come to everyone at some stage. Try instead to concentrate on the present – the next match, the next training session. The bigger picture will take care of itself and can be enjoyed in the rear-view mirror!

Tom Parsons
MAYO FOOTBALLER 2008-2021

Following a horror injury in 2018, Parsons was told he'd never run again, never mind make a comeback for Mayo. Despite being dropped from the panel in 2011, Parsons made a return, being recalled in 2014. These two instances alone show Parsons as one of the most resilient and hardest-working players in the country. He has won three u21 Connacht titles and four Connacht titles at senior level. With his club, Charlestown Sarsfields, he's won a Mayo SFC and a Mayo and Connacht Intermediate Championship. Tom is the current CEO of the GPA.

Who was your favourite player growing up?

Liam McHale, he was a fantastic midfielder for Mayo. As a kid I loved basketball as well, and Liam excelled in both sports.

What's your daily routine?

I start every day with some family time, with a ten-month-old baby, this time is precious. I work predominantly from home since the rise of Covid-19, so routine and habits are important. After work, I usually train; this is a mix of field-based training, or strength and conditioning. From 9pm I always, without fail, turn off my phone, read a book or watch some Netflix before bed at 10.30.

How many times do you train alone and with the team?

Usually three times a week with my team, and twice weekly by myself. Thursday is a recovery day, and although I don't train Saturday, I often do some video analysis, rehab or seek physio to keep the body in check.

How do you get rid of nerves before a game?

Exposure, experience and visualisation all help with nerves. The more we expose ourselves to high-pressure games, it helps build our resilience to deal with nerves or anxiety. Another great mindset method is visualisation, it's probably my favourite mindset tool.

You had a very serious knee injury in May of 2018 – how did you recover from that?

Many said I wouldn't return to play for Mayo. But determination, hard work and belief meant I did. For anybody struggling with injury, my advice is be patient, listen to your body, trust the professionals, and get to work. Your body will respond and heal when given the right environment, sleep, good food, de-stress and consistent rehab, I believe we can overcome all injuries.

Final advice in life is a quote I often read, 'Do what is hard and life will be easy, but do what is easy and life will be hard'. Never underestimate the power of hard work, positive mental attitude and trust in others.

Keep an open mind. Get better, try new things ...

Sarah Rowe
MAYO FOOTBALLER 2012-PRESENT

Denise Gaule

Mattie Donnelly

Declan O'Sullivan

odge Collins

THE HALF-FORWARDS' ADVICE

Neil McManus

Lyndsey Davey

Mattie Donnelly

TYRONE FOOTBALLER 2010-PRESENT

One of the best footballers in the country. He has played in almost every position during his time with the Red Hands (centre-back, midfield, half-forward, full-for-ward). Donnelly has won three Ulster titles, two All-Stars and represented Ireland in two International Rules Series.

Mindset and Lifestyle

Like all pillars discussed in this book, each of them depends on the other. Coming through the ranks, the biggest factors that determine a player's progress are the choices they make along the way. These choices are all driven by mindset. The mindset of the best players I have seen is ambitious, humble, determined and honest. Ambitious enough to push themselves to get the best out of themselves, whatever this might be. Determined enough to live a life of discipline and diligence. Humble enough to know that they can always learn, and always get better. Honest enough to know if they are working to the best of their ability.

Ambition to me is belief that you can get the best out of yourself, and that your best self can achieve great things. An ambitious person challenges themselves to compete at the highest level.

Determination, grit, resilience, whatever you want to call it, are all needed. Trying to achieve something will have many setbacks and chal-lenges. These will prevent you from throwing the towel in. They'll help you make the right decisions. Mental toughness is making the right decisions when no one is watching, time and time again.

Humility can take many forms. It's never getting ahead of yourself. Rec-ognising that the team and the jersey will always be bigger than yourself. It's also recognising that you can always get better. There is always some-thing you can improve. Can you pass with both feet and both hands? Can you tackle on both sides? There are endless questions we can ask of ourselves and humility is the raw ingredient that allows us to ask them.

Honesty is reviewing all of the above. When the thing hasn't gone the way you had planned, you'll look at yourself first, thoroughly. Are you doing the thing as well as you can? Am I a good team-mate? Ask yourself hard questions or get someone else to answer them for you.

Above all else, enjoy it.

Podge Collins
CLARE DUAL PLAYER 2012-PRESENT

One of the highest profile dual-players in the country, Collins has been an important player for the Banner in both codes. The 2013 All-Star had a successful underage career, winning a Munster minor title, two Munster u21 titles and two All-Ireland u21 Championships. With the seniors he has won a National League and an All-Ireland. He has also won two Clare Hurling Championships and two Clare Football Championships with his club Cratloe.

The advice I would give my younger self would be to focus on making individual training and team trainings as enjoyable as possible. Include games with friends and players to enhance skills away from the team environment. This can be done by doing shooting competitions or alley sessions.

I always had a keen interest in nutrition and how it impacted performance so I would just say to my younger self to diary what I felt worked on game days to create a clearer outline of what worked well for me.

With regards to gym, look to the experts for guidance. I would seek out S&C coaches that view conditioning as a whole. Focusing on mobility, strength and power to ensure injury prevention and sustainable performance are the priority.

Paul Finlay
MONAGHAN FOOTBALLER 2003-2016

Finlay will forever be remembered as a stalwart of Monaghan football. The playmaker lined out at both midfield and half-forward for the Farney men. During his career Finlay had great success, winning a Sigerson with Sligo IT, three National Leagues, two Ulster Championships and a Monaghan SFC with Ballybay Pearse Brothers.

There are many different aspects to achieving your maximum potential as a sportsperson no matter which sport you play. In Gaelic football, strength and conditioning, nutrition and keeping a general healthy lifestyle are all areas you will hear much about and rightly so. Strength, power and mobility are definitely important areas that need continuous improvement and development but I believe the basic skills of Gaelic football are not being practised enough by our young players.

Kicking accurately off both feet, catching the ball over your head and evading tackles are all the fundamentals of the game and those who can do these basics while running at speed and under pressure are those who succeed and go on to play at the highest level.

Securing possession while running at full speed and under pressure from an opponent, scoring a point in the closing minutes of a game when your team needs a score are the plays that win matches.

The higher your stats in these key areas the better chance you have of making it to the top.

Good luck.

Liam Óg McGovern
WEXFORD HURLER 2012-PRESENT

A highly versatile player, McGovern has lined out and starred at midfield, half-forward and full-forward. With his club, St Anne's Rathangan, he has won a Wexford Minor football championship, Wexford u21 Hurling Championship and a Wexford SFC. He has suffered and come back from two cruciate ligament injuries, to play a vital role in Wexford's Leinster Championship success in 2019.

Gym

Learning how to lift properly is more important than lifting heavy when starting off. Good technique is very important to maximise performance gains and reduce injury. Seek advice from people who are qualified and have your best interest at heart.

Nutrition

Educate yourself on food. Healthy eating is beneficial not just for sport performance, but for your overall health and well-being (energy, skin, mood, confidence etc). Once you start reaping the benefits of eating healthy, your outlook on food will change for the better. My advice is to start sooner rather than later.

Skill Practice

Practice doesn't make perfect, good practice makes perfection. Better to train for ten minutes at full pace putting yourself under pressure than to swan around aimlessly for hours. Focus exactly on what you want to improve, then execute over and over.

Disappointments / Rejection / Failure

Never nice, but part of life unfortunately. Everyone experiences them at some stage, but it's how you respond that really matters. This could be in sport, your studies or even with relationships. The temptation will be to give up, but it's important to train yourself to bounce back and try again. Perhaps even trying a slightly different approach the next time would make all the difference. It's like a muscle, the more you train it, the stronger it gets. Increasing your ability to bounce back will stand to you as you go through life!

Enda Smith
ROSCOMMON FOOTBALLER 2013-PRESENT

One of the first names on the Roscommon team sheet, Smith has shown time and time again to be a big-game player for them, winning a Sigerson with DCU, three National Leagues and two Connacht titles along the way. The Rossies' captain also represented Ireland in the 2017 International Rules Series.

Skill Development

This is probably the most important part of a Gaelic footballer and probably a hurler too. It possibly gets neglected a lot more these days as there is a big push on S&C, nutrition, rest and so on, which are all very important in their own right. However, for me, if you don't have the basic skills as you move towards the top level it is a much harder game to play.

Gym

An important aspect of the game that has come to prevalence in the last ten years. Personally, I probably wouldn't have been a big man for the gym, but in recent years have bought into it and can really see the benefits it has, especially when you are playing around the middle of the pitch.

Lifestyle and Nutrition

I'm all about getting the balance right when it comes to this side of the game. You can definitely overdo and overthink this, but you have to find what fits your own body the best. Some lads like to eat a lot before big games, others do not. It's important to find what works best for you and get into a routine of that.

Preparation

Without doubt I find sleep a key part of my own preparation these days. If I didn't get enough during the week, it's something that I would definitely feel at the weekend if I was training or playing a game. I like to get to bed at least one hour before midnight. If you are getting your seven to eight hours a night you won't go far wrong.

Denise Gaule
KILKENNY CAMOGIE PLAYER 2009-PRESENT

Arguably the best player in the country, Gaule has been marshalling the Cats' attack for the past decade. A two-time All-Ireland winner at minor, she first played for the seniors in an All-Ireland semi-final, a week after winning her second minor title. She later won the Young POTY award for that season. The two-time POTY (2016 and 2020) has won five National Leagues, two All-Irelands and four All-Stars.

Gym

I find when it comes to gym that getting into a routine is the biggest thing, I'm not a big fan of home workouts so I find having somewhere to go gives me the motivation to do the work. Having a programme to follow is a big help as you know exactly what has to be done on that day. I find the gym a good space for my mind and can benefit a lot more than just physically.

Nutrition

The nutritional aspect is what I find the hardest. I find exercising fine, but keeping on track with my food is a lot harder because I don't have great discipline. Again having a routine with work, keeping food simple and planning for the day ahead whether it's a training day or a rest day helps a lot.

Preparation

Preparation for training is all about organisation. I tend to go straight from work to training during the week so I need to ensure that my food is all prepared and my bag is ready the night before. Preparation also includes rest, recovery and mental preparation, particularly before a match. I think everyone's preparation is different, it's just about finding a routine and what works best for you. I try to keep my routine as consistent as I can, but it can change with regard to time of training/match. I'm a lot better at keeping the routine for match days, but again if the match is early/late or home/away routine can vary. I would be up early anyway and try to get out for a short walk in the morning and usually have a few pucks with my father out the back before heading off. I'd usually eat the same things: porridge, eggs and then pre-match meal usually pasta or a sandwich. I try to eat two hours before the game or training, but I know all the girls on the team differ. I wouldn't be too into the mental side of things, but I try to do a small bit of visualisation the night before games, just thinking back on good situations in the past and what was done well; I find this helps me! I'd be calm enough on match days and enjoy just having the chats and bit of craic. This is something I've learned over the years, but everyone is different – some people like listening to music or keeping to themselves. I used to think that's what I have to do, or it looks bad to be laughing before big games, but it definitely helps to keep me calm and relaxed.

Skill Enhancement

For me it's about challenging myself, whether at training or on my own. I try to use my bad side in most drills at training if I can. I believe to improve you need to find weaknesses and work on these whether in training or outside of it.

Advice to My Younger Self

As clichéd as it sounds, I'd say just enjoy it all and cherish all the moments and experiences that come into your life through sport. Win or lose, hard work pays off with all the teammates and friends you make along the way; at the end of the day, winning isn't everything.

Graham Geraghty
MEATH FOOTBALLER 1991-2012

An integral part of the Meath team of the 90s, Geraghty brought steel and toughness anytime he took to the pitch for the Royal County. An All-Ireland winning captain in 1999, his medal haul is enviable to say the least, winning one minor and two u21 Leinster championships, All Ireland minor and u21 titles, two National Leagues, three Leinster titles, two All-Irelands and two All-Stars, one Meath SFC, a Meath and Leinster Junior Championship and he also represented Ireland in three International Rules Series.

In today's modern game, gym work has become part and parcel of the Gaelic player's weekly routine. Players' physiques have changed and strength and conditioning is very important. During my career I did do some gym work but not to the extent we see now. For me, I have seen a lot of very good footballers who had loads of pace slow down as a result of too much gym work. While there is a place for strength and conditioning, we do need to get the right balance.

Nutrition again can be overdone, in my opinion. When I played, I ate what I wanted, really. I think if you're doing that much training and cardio work, you're burning off excess food you don't need. You need a good food supply to fuel the muscles, but I feel we don't need to be as strict as we are.

Lifestyle is a choice, some players are stricter on themselves than others. I remember different coaches over the years telling players there was a drink ban and so on. It's up to every individual, I certainly didn't stick to the rules all the time. Staying in and staying out of the limelight seems to be the thing now, although with Twitter, Instagram and Facebook it gets harder and harder to do that. Players know that when you become an inter-county player you give away a certain amount of your personal life to the public.

Preparation is down to each individual, but as a team we all met on the morning of games for breakfast, had a chat about the game and headed to the venue. All the hard work is done in the weeks coming up to the game, so it's all about trying to keep yourself occupied leading up to the match.

Skills enhancement is different for every player. Some players are born with God-given talents and others have to work hard to attain them. I believe that we can all improve. For example, in 1999 one of my coaches would hound me every session to kick with my left foot. He broke my heart to be honest. It did pay off that year, it got me out of a lot of trouble and I even scored some memorable points along the way to my second All-Ireland. So it does pay to learn new skills and to practise the ones we already have.

If I was to give advice to my younger self, it would be to stay in school, be true to yourself, be respectful of others and, of course, shut your mouth on the football field.

Diarmuid Lyng
WEXFORD HURLER 2004-2013

Gizzy was one of Wexford's most skilful hurlers, a versatile player who overcame obstacles both on and off the pitch. His medal haul includes two Leinster u21 titles, one National League and one Leinster Championship. He has also won two Wexford SHC with his club, St Martin's. He now works as a pundit with *Off the Ball*.

Advice to my younger self

Relax, you will get there. You will play in Croke Park.

You won't get your hands on the big one. But that's OK.

You'll play against the greats.

Shefflin will break your thumb. Kilkenny will break your heart. And Eoin Quigley will score the greatest point ever scored in Croke Park.

A physical trainer will walk into your dressing room and tell you about food.

They'll tell you that chicken is protein. That pasta is a carb. Before training it's carbs, with protein after to aid repair. You'll consider getting up to the dawn chorus during 'loading times' to eat steak in order to hit KPI's.

These terms will mean little to you.

So listen.

Savour your steak, but acknowledge the real sacrifice and eat less of it. Enjoy the sweetness of every tomato, apple and blackberry. Cherish the spud.

Eat dairy moderately.

Plant. Grow. Forage.

Cook with curiosity. The aromas, the flavours. Embrace them all as you engage in the moment-to-moment passing of the ceremony of sharing food.

Don't listen to anyone that reduces food to calories, carbs or proteins.

They've forgotten the interconnectedness of things.

The strands from which our stories are woven.

Paul Kerrigan

CORK FOOTBALLER 2008-2020

Kerrigan has won a raft of honours, including captaining Cork to three Munster u21 titles in 2005, 2006 and to an u21 All-Ireland title in 2007. He made his Senior debut in the 2008 Munster Final against Kerry, winning his first of three Munster titles. He won a Sigerson in 2009 with Cork IT. Kerrigan won his All-Ireland in 2010, operating as a key part of Cork's forward unit. He has also enjoyed a rake of success with his club, Nemo Rangers, winning four Munster Club Championships and seven Cork Club Championships. Kerrigan has also represented Ireland twice in the International Rules Series.

For me skill development is all about learning. I played minor for Cork in 2003 and I've been playing inter-county with Cork every year since. At thirty-two years of age I am still eager to enhance my skills. My advice for younger players is to learn by doing. Like anything, you will only get better at something if you WANT to get better. The key for me is simple – PRACTICE. Identify what you need to improve and put the time into it.

In my teens I played a lot of football and soccer, with many age groups. I made a lot of mistakes and maybe tried things that I didn't necessarily have the ability or skill to do. But that's OK, it's important to keep trying. If you are not putting in the time to practise, then you won't improve. Through effective skill-practice, you become more capable, competent, and confident in yourself and your performance, and are better able to reach your goals.

Generally when you think about improving or enhancing, you immediately think of working on your weaknesses or skills you're not that good at. You'll often hear coaches say 'practise kicking or hand passing off your bad side'. And that is vitally important. There have been many things I believed that I was not that good at and then spent a lot of time working on to try to improve them. Examples include tackling, fielding, hand passing for scores with my left hand. With practice I have improved in these areas.

But I think it's just as important to ensure you put in the time on your strong side, get unbelievably good at the basics on your good side. Think of Conor McManus of Monaghan who is right footed, he takes the frees on the right-hand side of the pitch and consistently scores. Usually people would say 'leave it to a left legger'. This is an example of someone who has put in huge hours on his 'good side' and has enhanced his kicking.

As a sixteen and seventeen-year-old I was on a club senior panel with two former Cork players – Colin Corkery and James Masters. In our club these were the two players who possessed the most skill and were the best at kicking and shooting. As a young forward I'd often go out kicking with these two. It was a brilliant learning experience and there's no doubt my skills and overall performance hugely improved from practising with these guys. They gave great advice and tips on shooting and free taking. Now I'm a free taker with my own team, and now as an older player I think it's important for me to put in the time with younger players and be available for advice should they want it. So your teammates and friends can be a great source of skill development.

The teenage years are a real growth period physically for players as they are going from kids to young adults. It's a time of great opportunity for players to grow their skills as well. This is a time for players to have fun and not take results too seriously. From my experience, whether you're twelve or thirty-two, I believe there can be great fun in improving and seeing yourself get better at something, not just in winning. Learning a new skill or under-going training will give you a sense of achievement; the whole process of learning can be very rewarding.

Fergal Conway
KILDARE FOOTBALLER 2014-PRESENT

A powerhouse around the middle third, Conway has lined out for the Lilywhites at centre-back, midfield and half-forward. A dual player with his club, Celbridge, he has won three Kildare SHC.

Nutrition

Very important aspect of sport. Helps with recovery after tough gym and pitch sessions. Nutritionists help give a guide on what players should eat daily depending on what their goal is.

Gym

Done every week, the weeks of important matches it won't be as hard. Focus is always trying to become stronger to help you play games, to break tackles and so on.

Skill Practice

The most important thing is to be able to perform the basic skills needed for your sport and constant practice is needed.

Mindset:

Always have a positive mindset to help you overcome difficult games or injuries.

Lifestyle

Doing things to help you perform to your best! Sleep, eating the right food and controlling the things you can control.

Preparation

Making sure you have eaten good food to fuel you for games or training and also to help you recover. Make sure to have football boots at the ready along with your kit.

Advice to my younger self

Don't be afraid to make mistakes!

Amy O'Connor
CORK CAMOGIE PLAYER 2014-PRESENT

An underage soccer international, O'Connor made it to the semi-finals of the u19 European Championships, but when the time came to make a decision there was only ever going to be one winner. She has since won four All-Ireland titles with the Rebelettes. The Cork captain followed her All-Star in 2019 with a POTM performance in the All-Star game, scoring 3-5.

The advice I would give to my younger self is:

•Enjoy playing as much sport as you can for as long as you can.
•Do your best in school – and that doesn't mean getting straight A's. All you can do is your best.
•Don't settle for something just because that has always been the norm – break the cycles that have gone before you. Just because it hasn't already been done, doesn't mean it can't be done.
•Spend as much time with your family as you possibly can and enjoy every moment of it.
•Be kind and caring and never exclude anyone from anything, no matter what it is. Always make people feel involved.
•If I was growing up in today's generation I would say spend as little time as possible on social media and your phone!

Declan O'Sullivan
KERRY FOOTBALLER 2003-2014

When we talk about centre-forward play, O'Sullivan is without a doubt one of the best players to watch and replicate. In his final season he lined out in the Munster final with both knees heavily strapped, taking up a 'quarter-back' role spraying passes across the full-forward line. An out-and-out leader, over the course of his career he claimed five All-Irelands with the Kingdom two of them as captain in back-to-back seasons, three NFLs, six Munster titles, five Kerry Championships and three All-Stars. He is the current Kerry u20 manager.

Gym

I was never a huge fan of gym work during my career, but it has become essential now for any footballer looking to compete at inter-country level. Some of the basic tips I would give are:

Seek advice from qualified instructors.

Follow a pre-planned programme, which is designed to help you become a better, more durable all-round footballer. That is the only objective; is the work I'm doing in the gym making me a better footballer? Do not lose sight of that.

Make sure to get your technique correct before introducing heavy weight.

Concentrate on flexibility and injury-prevention exercises like stretching, core exercises, band work and using your own body weight for strength work. Using your own body weight means you can do strength work whenever and wherever you want, which leads to a more flexible and sustainable plan in the long term.

Nutrition

Eat a good breakfast every day. It is so easy to get into a habit of rushing out the door every morning without eating. You have not eaten in ten or twelve hours, so your body needs fuel.

Get into good eating habits the week of a game, particularly the day or two before a game where you should aim to load up to give your body the energy it requires to perform at its highest level.

Eat as soon as possible after training/game to help yourself recover for the next training/game.

Hydrate well every day. Get into the habit of sipping water throughout the day.

Learn how to cook. This will stand to you when you move away from home to study/work. Processed foods or take-aways are not a good option if you want to play good football.

I would encourage a natural approach to your diet, rather than supplements.

PREPARATION

Develop a routine for match weeks. Interactions regarding the upcoming game should be limited to people within your circle. Talking about the game to too many people will lead to mental fatigue.

Prepare yourself mentally for the game ahead by visualising scenarios, which may happen in the game and how you would react to such situations. Have three or four key aims going into the game. Keep these aims simple and relatively consistent based on your role within the team. I liked to go for a walk by myself the night before or the morning of a game to talk these things through in my head. Positive self-talk is crucial.

There are certain non-negotiable requirements for every game you play so prepare to bring these traits every day.

100 per cent effort

Try your very best at all times regardless of what role you are asked to play, regardless of what form you are in, regardless of what team or manager you are playing for. I read an article where Irish runner Ciara Mageean said when she ran, she knew she was trying as hard as she could because she could taste blood in her mouth. That is a good trigger for players when they are preparing for games. You should prepare to run with the taste of blood in your mouth.

Body language

Positive body language, even when things are not going according to plan, react well to setbacks and try your best to turn things around in your team's favour. The best players are the ones who can turn their /or their team's performance around mid-game.

Team first

Do not let your ego get in the way of the team's objectives.

SKILL PRACTICE
Ball work

Keep working on your handling. Good handling gives you extra time. Securing possession and controlling the ball should be so natural that it allows you to get your head up and see what is happening around you in the game. This comfort on the ball requires hours and hours of ball work from a young age. Often this work is done on your own using a wall to perfect your catching, kicking and your reaction skills.

Two-sided player

It is such an advantage if you can kick and hand pass off both sides. It becomes very difficult for an opposition player to anticipate what you are going to do if you have this ability. I developed my right side much later than I should have, but it improved my game so much. What helped me develop my weaker leg was kicking a ball soccer-style off a wall and kicking it back with whichever leg it rebounded to. It really helped my mind to be more natural and instinctive off my right side.

Fitness

No matter how talented you are, it is still difficult to execute the skills to the best of your ability if you are tired. Make sure you are in good physical shape, which will ensure your talent gives you an advantage.

Advice to my younger self

Baz Luhrmann released an album in 1997 which contained the song 'Everybody's Free (To Wear Sunscreen)'. I was fourteen at the time and the song contained lots of brilliant advice, but one line in particular stuck with me and I have always carried it with me throughout my career.

'Don't waste your time on jealousy;
sometimes you're ahead, sometimes you're behind.
The race is long, and in the end, it's only with yourself'

In a football context in your early to mid-teens, football becomes competitive. Outside of your own club, you start playing schools football and divisional football with players from different clubs. During this period, there will be stages where football is going well and you think you have all the answers, other times when things aren't going well you can get disheartened and lose confidence. You and all the players around you are developing differently both physically and mentally. Dealing with the ups and downs during this period can be difficult. My advice is to just keep doing your best. Keep trying to improve and take on board the coach's advice. Enjoy your football, people play their best football when they don't overthink it and play with confidence in their own ability.

Your football journey is unique and success should be reaching *your* full potential, whatever level that may be, sharing that journey with great people and ideally a bit of silverware thrown in along the way.

Martin Clarke

AFL FOOTBALLER 2007-2009, 2012-2015
DOWN FOOTBALLER 2010-2011, 2015-2016

Following a successful minor career, Clarke was scouted by AFL club Collingwood. He enjoyed a run of form down under, earning him an AFL Rising Star nomination in 200. At the end of 2009, Clarke retired from the AFL, returning home to inspire Down to the All-Ireland final in 2010. His honours include an All-Ireland minor title, an u21 Ulster title and an All-Star award in 2010.

With more and more emphasis on strength and conditioning within the GAA, we are seeing a lot of the same type of player. Wonderfully rounded athletes, men and women who do most things very well.

There is no doubt it is essential to invest large amounts of time and energy into gym work, running sessions, game plan education, game management etc. Without a sound foundation in all those areas, you will struggle to get a game in a top club or county side.

Notwithstanding this, I would urge younger players to become elite at something. Stand out at something. Aim to be the best in your team, in your county, in your province, in the GAA at something.

For me it was all about my left-foot kicking. I am naturally right-handed and I rarely used my right foot, as I would hand pass my way out of trouble if I couldn't get onto my left foot. I could have spent months and years working to improve my right-foot kicking, but instead I invested this time to further improve my main strength, left-foot kicking. I would take a football with me everywhere, I'd be the first on the training field and last to leave, all my extra work was to refine my biggest strength. I felt for a couple of seasons in the early 2010s my ability to utilise my left-foot kicking skills allowed my club and county teams to have success.

So, I suppose the takeaway message from me would be to make your biggest assets shine rather than your major weaknesses hold you back.

Lyndsey Davey
DUBLIN FOOTBALLER 2004-PRESENT

Davey first played senior for Dublin when she was just fourteen years old. While in college she won three O'Connor Cups with DCU. A stalwart of the Jackies',, the six-time All-Star has won two National Leagues, thirteen Leinster titles, five All-Irelands and was named POTM in the 2019 All-Ireland final.

Trying to organise a work, training, life balance is difficult enough for most amateur athletes but when your job involves shift work it can make things a little more challenging. For me, the biggest difficulty is scheduling; seeing where work overlaps with training and then trying to arrange swaps and paying back shifts on my days off. When you're training four to five times a week, organising swaps can be time consuming and stressful, however, as is the case for most things in life, preparation and planning is key. I'm also extremely lucky to work with a great bunch of people who understand the level of commitment needed to play inter-county football and I probably wouldn't be able to play for Dublin if it wasn't for their help covering my shifts.

When working and training on the same day you need to be really organised and prepared to ensure you have all your work and football gear with you, on top of all the food that you need for the day. One of the benefits of working in a fire station, from a nutritional aspect, is that we have a fully equipped kitchen so I can cook all my meals fresh every day. I found this to be one of the more challenging aspects of working a nine to five roster, when I worked in the financial industry, as I would have to have all my meals pre-prepared before I left for work in the morning.

It can also be physically and mentally draining working a twelve-hour shift, day or night, and then going straight to training after. This is why it is so important to maximise rest and recovery on your days off. One of the advantages of shift work is the amount of time you have off. I'm fortunate enough to get eight days off in a row once a month. This time off allows me to catch up with friends and family and to enjoy a bit of time switching off from football and work which is very important for your mental wellbeing.

I love working as a firefighter and playing football for Dublin. It takes a lot of commitment and at times can be tough, but when you're lining out in Croke Park on the biggest day of the year representing your family, club and County, I know I wouldn't have it any other way.

Neil McManus
ANTRIM HURLER 2007-PRESENT

A successful underage career saw McManus win two Ulster Minor Hurling championships and two Ulster u21 Hurling Championships. With the seniors the Antrim ace has won a National League, ten Ulster Hurling Championships and a Joe McDonagh Cup. He has also won six Antrim Club Championships and four Ulster Club Championships with his club, Cushendall Ruairí Óg.

S&C, nutrition and lifestyle are the areas that prepare you for top level sport. Not only physically, but mentally. Mental toughness comes from knowing you have the work done. It's like a checklist within your own mind. Do I have a tick against all my areas of preparation? You have total control over these areas, so it's up to you to tick the box.

I put in extra hours outside of collective training for two reasons.

1. I love playing this sport.
2. I want to become the best player I can possibly be.

My additional work is mainly free-taking practice, gym work and recovery. Free taking is as much a mental challenge as a physical one and confidence is a must. Confidence for me comes from having my routine locked down and striking the ball cleanly – these need to be practised constantly.

Being in the best physical condition I can be allows me to enjoy the battle and thrive when the going gets tough.

There's nothing better than getting into the sea at the shore of Cushendall to enjoy the natural recovery the sea provides to our muscles and aches. I find it is also great for clearing my head and resetting back to normal after a match.

The advice I would give my younger self would be to choose what you want and go after it. Make sure it's your passion and follow it with all your heart.

No day is wasted following the passion of your life!

Seán Powter
CORK FOOTBALLER 2016-PRESENT

A Cork minor hurling and football championship winner with Douglas, Powter furthered his underage success, winning an u21 Munster Championship with the Rebels. Since his debut he has shown to be highly versatile, lining out at corner-back, half-back and centre-forward. He represented Ireland in the 2017 International rules series. He was nominated for young POTY the same season.

Nutrition

I'm a pretty basic eater, so I'll just take you through a normal day of eating for me.

Breakfast is porridge with a fistful of granola, or if I'm in a rush three Weetabix.

Snack: At about 11am I'd have a few pieces of pineapple with a small bag of popcorn to get me over to lunch time.

Lunch: Depends on whether it's a training day or rest day. On training I would usually have a chicken wrap with orange juice. If it was a rest day, I would grab a salad from the local shop.

Before training: I always have a chicken curry no matter what type of training session it is.

Post training: A protein shake straight after training for recovery.

Before bed: If the training session was tough enough, I would treat myself to a bit of ice cream or a small chocolate bar.

Gym

The aim of gym work is to improve your performance on the pitch and to prevent injuries. Too many people nowadays are going on programmes given by unqualified people on Instagram who have no history of your body and what parts of your body needs work, so it's extremely important for you to see a qualified strength and conditioning coach. 'Big biceps won't kick the ball over the bar.'

Skill Development

When I was younger, I was extremely weak off my left leg and once I started playing with the Cork Seniors, I was found out pretty quickly. So over the past three or four years I've spent ten minutes each day outside against my wall just kicking left leg only. It's not perfect yet, but with just ten minutes a day I have seen a dramatic improvement.

Mindset

Playing football for Cork is what I've always wanted to do. The mind-set I have always had since I was a young boy is that nobody will outwork me. Whether it was fitness runs, skills tests or just practising frees with my friends, I always wanted to win and if I lost, I would practise to ensure I wouldn't lose again.

Lifestyle

If you want to play for your county, you need to act like a county player. This includes who your friends are. 'You are who you hang around with' really is true. I had friends when I was younger who had no interest in GAA, but loved drinking and staying out late, playing Xbox and things like that. I quickly realised that these people weren't going to help me play for Cork. The friends I have now all support me and help me become the best player I can be.

Advice to younger self

One thing I would tell my younger self is to enjoy it more. When you're going training, just enjoy it. I've experienced a number of injuries recently and I've learnt how much I miss playing football when I am out injured. Finally, practise. Text your friend, make your dad go to the pitch or just go find a wall and kick. You'll be surprised how much a difference ten minutes a day can make.

Vikki Wall
MEATH FOOTBALLER 2014-PRESENT

A powerful runner, some might say when Wall gets the ball, she'll either be fouled or score. An integral part of Meath's recent success, a Player of the Match performance in the 2020 All-Ireland Final saw Wall inspire her side to victory. She followed it up with a National League title. The 2020 Intermediate POTY has also won a Meath Junior Championship, Leinster Junior championship, All-Ireland Junior Club championship. Meath Intermediate Championship, Leinster Intermediate Championship, All-Ireland Intermediate Club Championship and a Meath Senior Championship with her club, Dunboyne.

Gym

Gym and S&C programmes that I've been given have improved hugely over the last three years. Get a gym partner and keep it consistent.

Nutrition

I think it's important to get to know your own body; eating something before a game might work for you, even if it might not work for everyone else.

Lifestyle

As much as football is important and is such a major part of my life, I think it's good to have an identity outside of football. Trying to find a balance and making time for family, friends and things I enjoy makes me appreciate and love football much more.

Preparation

Trial and error for what works for you before a match is key. I always feel less pressure playing matches where I know I've trained well and know I've put everything into the process.

Skill

Don't underestimate the basic skills; you can never practise them too much.

Advice to my younger self

Don't be so hard on yourself – and practise on your 'other' foot sooner, could save you a lot of trouble.

Derek McNicholas

WESTMEATH HURLER 2004-PRESENT

McNicholas has lined out for the Lake County in a variety of positions such as half-back, half-forward and full-forward. During his long career with Westmeath he has won four National Leagues, three Christy Ring Cups, a Joe McDonagh Cup and a Westmeath SHC with his club, Lough Lene Gaels, and represented Ireland in three composite rules series. He has also won multiple individual accolades including Player of the Month in July 2016, Christy Ring All-Star, Joe McDonagh All-Star and a Fitzgibbon team of the year.

My advice to any young hurler who's really passionate about playing at the highest level is to make sure you develop strength correctly. S&C training can help with developing, but only if it is done correctly. If someone is further on in their development, don't force yourself to lift heavy weights and risk an injury that might affect you years down the road. Stretching regularly will definitely prolong your career in your later playing years.

When you leave secondary school and head to college, further education or training make sure you're happy with it. It's important to look after what you're doing off the field.

As an adult, aim to have a good job; don't do something that has you in the position just because of your inter-county status. When you are retired the new kid on the block will be the one who is the talk of the town and you might be forgotten about. It's very important you enjoy college and inter county/club hurling, but make sure you have some qualifications, so you can have a good job that you are happy in and financially secure for the future.

Jason Doherty
MAYO FOOTBALLER 2011-PRESENT

A highly versatile player, Doherty has played in a range of roles within Mayo's forward line. Whether he's operating as a linkman on the opposition's 40 or playing inside, he'll find a way to cause problems. Following strong displays at minor, Doherty continued to star at u21-level winning two Connacht titles. A Sigerson winner with DIT, Doherty has also won a National League and five Connacht Championships.

Gym

In relation to gym and strength work my main advice would be to take advice off experts only. Gym work can often be perceived as just lifting weights to get bigger and stronger. Performing on the pitch involves far more than just being strong. For younger players, the key emphasis should be on optimising technique and nailing the basics so when the time comes to lift weights, you can achieve maximum results.

Nutrition

Nutrition is another massively important aspect of performance, but equally it's crucial for your own health and fitness in general. Again, I would seek help and guidance from experts in the area of nutrition rather than guessing. Having a good diet can sometimes be mistaken for eating less so you don't put on weight, but the focus should be on eating smarter and eating higher quality food.

Lifestyle

In terms of lifestyle, these years should be about enjoying yourself. You will more than likely be in secondary school which means you will be making new friends, meeting new people and exposed to all sorts of temptations. This is a time in your life you have to be very disciplined with the situations and people you surround yourself with. Surround yourself with people who bring out the best in you and motivate you to become a better person.

Preparation

This is one area that looking back I would have given more attention to particularly in my later teens. It's a few small things like planning your week to know what you need to do and where you need to be, that can really make life a bit easier. Some simple goal setting is a great way to focus the mind and ensure each training has measurable success for you individually.

Skill Practice

It's a cliché, but the simple and most effective advice here is to practise, practise, practise. You cannot underestimate the power of effective practice. Some advice I would have here would be to look honestly in the mirror and make your practice effective by making it sport and/or match specific (e.g. practise what you will need to be able to do in competition).

Advice for my younger self

It would probably be to ask my coaches more questions, be more vocal and confident in group settings and care less about the outcome and focus more on the process and improving myself continuously.

Fintan Kelly
MONAGHAN FOOTBALLER 2013-PRESENT

Making his debut at corner back, Kelly has shown great versatility, playing in every line for the Farney Men since winning two Ulster Titles and picking up an All-Star nomination in 2017.

Nutrition

Educate yourself on the basics of nutrition. Try to get all your nutritional needs in with whole foods. Leave the supplements until you're older.

Gym

If your club provides a Strength and Conditioning coach buy into it and get learning how to move. The better you know how to move the easier it will be to stick to a gym programme in the future

Skill Development

If it's football you play and you want to get better, get yourself a ball and find a wall and repeat all the skills of the game as much as you can. Challenge yourself with skill challenges and try to beat your score each time. Same applies for any sport. Make sure you're enjoying what you're doing.

Mindset, lifestyle preparation

Enjoy every minute of your sport. If you want to get better, practise more. If you don't, just go out and enjoy yourself. Respect your club and its volunteers. Believe in yourself!

Advice to younger self

Be yourself!

David Treacy
DUBLIN HURLER 2009-PRESENT

A dual player at minor, Treacy won Leinster football and Hurling Championships. Following u21 success winning a Leinster Hurling Championship, he was called into the senior ranks, winning a National League and Leinster Championship. With his club, Cuala, he has won five Dublin SHC, two Leinster Club Championships and two Club All-Irelands.

Preparation

For me, preparation has been the key to any success I have had as a player.

Growing up, I used to get incredibly nervous ahead of games. It is only now, through my experience, that I have really settled around matches and this has been solely due to how I prepare for them.

In my teen years, I never really bought into preparation in advance of games and trusted that whatever would happen, would happen. It was only really when I reached minor level that the sport demanded me to prepare properly and it made the difference that helped me perform at a higher level. I wish I had taken it more seriously growing up while I was part of development squads.

Preparation can come in many forms. I've found that if I take care of as many controllables as possible, I can take comfort in the fact that I have done everything to allow me to perform. This could be as simple as getting my gear together in advance of a game, eating the same food at the same time before games, making sure my hydration is right. If I am taking frees, to ensure that I have taken twenty or thirty the day before. All of these factors allow me to believe that I have the work done and give me confidence when lining out.

This has now gradually moved on to the more mental side of the game. At inter-county level, everyone has similar levels of fitness, ability, strength and nutrition, but where there is a lot of headroom to grow is the mental aspect of how you prepare for a game.

In summary, making sure you take the time to properly prepare for each game both mentally and physically can transform how you approach the game and will improve you as an overall player. Everyone's preparation is personal to them and my advice would be to try different methods of preparation to find out what works best for you.

Eimear Scally

CORK FOOTBALLER 2014-PRESENT

Scally first played senior for her club, Éire Óg, at just thirteen years of age. At seventeen she was called into the Cork senior team while still starring for the minor side in their all-Ireland success. While in college she won an O'Connor Cup with UL. Scally has enjoyed great success with the Rebelettes, winning five National Leagues, five Munster titles and three All-Irelands.

From a young age, practising skills at football training and at home with my family or just by myself using the wall was very beneficial to me. It might have been minor improvements that were being made every time I went out, but they all added up for when games came around and I needed to put these skills to use. Doing simple things such as trying to better myself each time by playing 'keepie uppies' or trying to aim for the same spot on the wall all helped to having that bit of skill on the pitch.

It's very important that the joy of playing sports is kept, because once you stop enjoying it, the want to improve skills and improve yourself goes out the window. For me, I was always a 'tomboy' growing up, so I always wanted to be playing with the boys and playing sport, as the girls didn't play as much. Now, I feel the participation in ladies' sport has risen hugely and a lot of younger girls are just as competitive as the boys. All the media coverage has definitely helped.

Even though I feel my skill is good and at a level to play senior football for Cork, I continue to do extra practice with other players most days before/after training and that mainly includes practising free kicks and taking some penalties too. All of this practice can end up being the extra bit that gets you over the line. For me, finding that routine is important when taking a free or penalty, it helps focus your mind and also helps to relax you, especially if you're a nervous type of player. To be doing something as simple as taking a solo and a hop of the ball before you take a free could help just even that little bit. Along with that, the technique must be followed through.

On the technique, it's important that with kicking, soloing and hand-passing, the technique is executed perfectly before you move onto more complex skills. Being able to execute all the main things that you need to do in football can make you a very good player without being able to do the complex stuff such as kicking a ball from the outside of your boot from the sideline.

Once all these skills are up to a very good standard, it's great to be able to practise the tougher skills such as the dummy solo, outside of the boot kicking and so on. The practice of these skills needs to be religious and done a few times a week even just by yourself, the time is there in the week to get it done. For me, going out to have a few kicks by myself is still enjoyable, I want to be one of the best every time I go out on the pitch so in order for this to happen, I need to practise loads and thankfully, it's what I love.

Enjoyment and practice are key words that I've mentioned throughout, so I think it's key for any players who aspire to improve to remember these things for football.

Oisín McConville
ARMAGH FOOTBALLER 1994-2008

Without a doubt one of Armagh's greatest ever players, McConville is one of the deadliest forwards the game has produced, contributing from frees and open play. During his time with the Orchard County, he won a National League, seven Ulster Championships and an All-Ireland. At club level, the Armagh legend has won sixteen Armagh SFC and ten Ulster club SFC, six club All-Irelands with Crossmaglen. The two-time All-Star now works as a pundit on *The Sunday Game*.

What inspired you to play football?

I grew up in the troubles; bombings and shootings were commonplace in my area. Gaelic football was a strong part of the community. My family were heavily involved in Crossmaglen, my brothers all played for the club, Dad was involved, and Mum was the secretary for years. Me playing football was a natural progression. There were no other sports around, no rugby or soccer, purely football. When I first picked up a ball, I loved it. From that moment on I never stopped kicking.

How would you prepare for a big game?

I would always make sure I had everything right the week before a big match. First thing would be that I'd eat as close to right as I could. Plenty of good rest too. On the day of the game I would be nervous so I would eat whatever I could keep down during the day. As long as I got good rest earlier in the week, I knew I'd be okay. If your preparation is right it gives you the best possible opportunity to perform. Avoid overtraining and always stay hydrated.

How did you practise frees?

The big thing was routine. I would only ever take ten free kicks. Dave Alred, Johnny Wilkinson's kicking coach, did a session with us on a training camp. He spoke about the danger of over kicking, that players are better off practising taking a few quality kicks than multiple okay ones. Quality over quantity. This stayed with me throughout my career. After that when it came to frees, I kept plugging away. I used to keep a log of frees that I took and then chart the improvement or reassess if there was a decline. I would try to kick each one the same, as if my life was on the line with every kick. I'd kick four or five times a week, after training and one night away from it on my own. Find a routine that works for you and stick to it.

How do you keep your head up when you make a mistake?

You'll never play a perfect game, you'll miss frees, get turned over etc. One of my underage managers told me this. After that I used to make sure I kept telling myself I would make mistakes. Once I realised this, I was never as hard on myself. I missed a penalty in an All-Ireland final. Through being in the right mental state of knowing I would make a mistake, I was able to come back out after halftime and score a goal. Pick up a bit of grass and throw it away. That's the mistake done with, move on, next ball.

Did you ever get nervous before games? How did you handle it? Should players try to get rid of nerves?

When I was younger, nerves weren't really prevalent. As I got older that's when I started to get more nervous. The way I dealt with it was, I embraced them. For me nerves were natural, something that I needed. When I got nervous, I knew it meant it was a big game. I tried to turn them into a positive. Be aware and careful that nerves can cripple you before a match. The way I spun it, I felt I was able to make nerves help my performance.

It's never too late

You're never too old to learn new tricks. If I use the example of Ryan Giggs, when he first came to the fore at Manchester United, he predominantly used his pace. By the time he was thirty-three or thirty-four, naturally he wasn't as fast as he once was. In order to tease out another four or five years of his career, he taught himself new tricks, he learned to play different positions, to take up different roles in order to keep playing the game he loved.

Off the Pitch

If you're happy away from football it's easier to be happy on the pitch. I was on the pitch with my own demons and it's much harder to try to play with them. I had to overcome these demons in order to be happier in training, happier in matches, happier. If there's something bothering you, the best thing is to share it with someone else. Football is as much a mental game as it is a physical one.

Ciara McAnespie

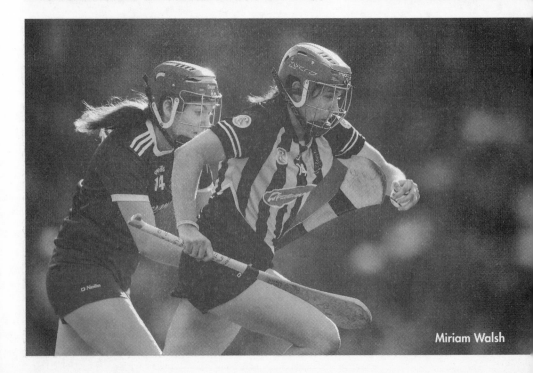

Miriam Walsh

Kieran Donaghy

John Mullane

THE FULL-FORWARDS' ADVICE

Conor Cooney

Ross Munnelly

Eddie Brennan
KILKENNY HURLER 2000-2012

Having never played minor for Kilkenny, Brennan first played with the Cats at u21 level, winning a Leinster and All-Ireland Championship. Over the next decade, he would go on to have a massively successful career, winning five National Leagues, eleven Leinster titles and eight All-Irelands. The four-time All-Star has also won two Kilkenny SHC, Leinster Club Championship, and Kilkenny and Leinster Intermediate Club Championship with his club, Graigue-Ballycallan. In the winter of 2018, the Kilkenny legend was ratified as Laois manager. During his time with the O'Moore men he won a Joe McDonagh Cup.

Monday would have involved some form of recovery or a gym session after a Sunday training session, so Monday morning recovery, good food eaten during the day, what your body needs to recover. I was never massively obsessed with specific food. I think if you're getting your meat, veg and carbs, be it potatoes or whatever, that's going to keep you right. It doesn't have to be pasta, pasta, pasta all the way, which I think maybe some of us thought was the only way.

Tuesday I would have had the gear bag packed from the night before. That's the most important part of being prepared because you just don't know what's going to happen in work maybe or what's going to happen with traffic, so the last thing you need is having to go home and collect stuff. I would have always had a backup set of gear left in the boot of the car as well. Realise everything you do on the training pitch is being watched, it counts towards you making the team.

Wednesday was another recovery day, maybe a good pool session or stretching at home, foam rolling. I was living in Portlaoise at the time, so the ball alley out in Clannad was a place where I'd go when we didn't have team sessions. We'd train three nights a week, so I'd do the guts of forty minutes every other evening in the ball alley or if not, just a wall close to the house.

Thursday Maybe get another ball-wall session done just charging up the batteries and get a good stretch session in. It's impossible not to think about the game on Sunday. Other than the few pucks and stretches I would try not to think about the match. Whether it be going shopping for the day with my other half or a five to six kilometre walk with the dog through Emo woods; anything to get my mind off it, but obviously the game was never too far from my mind.

Friday's training session again, get your food right on the day, so you're eating a good dinner around lunchtime and then at about 4:00 o'clock maybe a sandwich or something like that. It was part of the routine, the habits that I knew had me properly fuelled up for training. Maybe have a few snacks in the car just to keep you tipping over and obviously loads of water. Friday's training session would have always been heavy enough, so leave Saturday as another recovery day and then into the match on Sunday.

Match day, my routine never changed much. I'd get up early around 7-7:30, go for a walk listening to my iPod, which is a blast from the past now. We had a trampoline out the back, so I'd have a few bounces on that to get myself fired up. Everything ready from the night before. The bus was always relaxed with a bit of craic too. As we got closer to the stadium the more I'd think about the match. I'd do my own thing once inside, go out to the pitch, get a feel for the atmosphere and the conditions. I'd go somewhere quiet on my own to do my stretches and ball work which in Croke Park happened to be the showers. The ultimate goal for a match-day routine is that it's a familiar process. Early on in your career you don't think of this as it's only when you're playing that bit longer and have a couple of bad days that you look for these edges. Nerves are a good thing. You want to walk into a game knowing you have the work done, built up over a number of weeks and training sessions, being ready to go.

For me a big thing with psychological preparation was analysing opponents in your own time. We never did a huge amount of collective analysis on opposition, never had analysis packs sent to us on opposition players. I felt it was my responsibility to look at weaknesses/strengths of guys that'd be marking you. More importantly you need to focus on yourself. Visualise situations you're likely to be in in a match. Think of these scenarios and ask how do I react? If I'm beaten to the first two balls, how do I react? If there's no ball coming in to me, how do I get myself into the match? Get a hook, get a block, win a ruck, whatever. On match day you need to feel ready and relaxed, but also on edge. Look forward to the match and realise you have all the hard work done.

Ross Munnelly
LAOIS FOOTBALLER 2003-PRESENT

When it comes to longevity, very few players come close to Munnelly. His motivation remains to go as hard as he can for as long as he can. For the past two decades he has been Laois's go-to-man. He has won a Leinster Championship, a Laois SFC and represented Ireland in three International Rules Series.

While I was between the ages of twelve and fifteen years old, I found it very difficult to make my club teams at these age grades. It was a very disheartening and frustrating time for me. I grew up across the road from my old primary school, and when I would arrive home from a game having not really played I would drop my gear bag, take out my boots and some footballs and go straight across the road to the school pitch.

To help get over the disappointment of not playing the game, I would practise until I was called home for dinner. As a forward, my coach always told me to practise kicking the ball high, but with an easy strike. As I got older, I could kick it further and further without having to kick it hard. This was some of the best advice I ever received – kick the ball high, but with a smooth and easy strike; I still practise this today.

By the age of fifteen, I was starting to make a breakthrough, I made the Laois u16 squad and quickly realised how important it was to catch the ball first time. This meant I had an extra second or two before a defender could tackle me. I started kicking the ball off the wall at home and in school, kicking harder and harder so the ball would be rebounding harder than a kick pass in a game. When I got comfortable at this from a standing position, I then practised while running towards the wall to meet the rebounding ball. This was even harder to do, but in time it really helped me in game situations when the players out the field would kick the ball in long and I was comfortable collecting that pass at full pace. Again, this gave me a slight advantage where I could make a pass or take a shot before the defender was able to tackle me.

From twelve to eighteen years old I went to see so many club and county games around Laois and Croke Park. I would learn about players and try to copy some of the skills and decisions those players made in the big matches. Then when I was training, I would focus on doing the same things. Learning from watching others continues to be something I really enjoy, every game, every week, I see something to improve on and an area where I can be better. No matter who you are or how long you are playing, you can always improve and play to a higher standard. It takes practice!

John Mullane
WATERFORD HURLER 2001-2012

A real fan favourite, Mullane will forever be remembered as an icon. During his time with Waterford he won a National League and four Munster Championships. The five-time All-Star led from the front, with a mix of passion and scoring prowess he was a handful for any defender. The Déise legend has also won three Waterford SHC and two Munster Club Championships with De La Salle.

How old were you when you knew you wanted to play for Waterford?

You always dream of wanting to hurl for Waterford. The reality was probably in 1998, going to watch Waterford. They had a very good run that year, got to the league final, got to the Munster final, got to the All-Ireland semi-final and were beaten by Kilkenny. It was just a magical summer, France '98, the World Cup was on, the first Munster final Waterford were in since '89. Just going to the matches, it was the height of the Celtic Tiger, always 45-50 thousand at every match. Being up on the terraces in Thurles, Pairc Uí Chaoimh and Croke Park, I said, 'There's one day I'd love to push on and play at that level, play in front of the big crowds.' Lo and behold, three or four years later it finally came true, I got my break. Played minor in '99, u21 in 2000, called into the senior panel in 2001 and never looked back. I would've played Tony Forrester in 1994 on the B team, I was on the A team in '95. I probably wasn't a stand-out player until I got to minor under Jim Greene, then I had a bit of self-belief that I was good enough to push on and play senior hurling one day.

What's the best piece of advice you received during your career?

To keep going to the end. It's something that was drilled in from when I was younger right through to adult, to keep going to the final whistle, no matter what the scoreboard was, never drop the head, always play to the final whistle. It was probably the best advice I ever got, regardless of what the scoreline was on the day of a match, whether you're ahead or behind or getting well beaten in a match. You don't down the tools, you just keep going; if other lads are being beaten around you, you just keep going to the end. It's a good trait to have, to build up that way in your mindset that no matter what happens today, no matter what the scoreboard is, I'm just going to keep hurling until the end. I think that's something that stood me in good stead during the course of my career.

How do I keep my head up when I make a mistake?

An awful lot of that comes from experience. Tony Browne always used to say it's all about the ball, nothing else matters, it's just about the ball. Early on in my career, if I missed a ball or I wasn't getting on ball, I probably would have dealt with it badly, a small bit of frustration. As the years went on I would've learned to be patient, if you weren't getting on a ball or missed a ball. You'll get a five-minute spell, you'll get a ten-minute spell and you'll do damage within that period.

Playing corner-forward, you had to be patient. It wasn't like today's game where you can get on a load of possessions. Back then, corner forward, you might've seen eight, nine, ten possessions in a game, the player that's marking you might win three, four or five. It's about what you can do with the other five or six possessions, that ultimately decides what you're going to do in a game. You might win a couple of frees, could end up scoring 1-2 or 1-3 off the remaining possessions.

An awful lot of it would be patience. If I missed a ball it was always the case that I was going to win the next one.

How do I deal with sledging?

I would've experienced a fair bit over the years. Some of it, you kind of have to give as good as you get. Nothing stupid, but that you wouldn't let your opponent walk all over you, to stand up for yourself.

More of it is the psychological part. The way to overcome sledging in any environment is to win that individual battle. Constantly beating that player up on the scoreboard, winning frees or just winning more ball against him. Keeping that scoreboard going, because that's what will really hurt him; putting the ball over the bar, winning frees or setting up scores.

How would you prepare for a big game?

I would have had all the hard work done up to the week of a match. Tuesday sessions, I would go full on, all in for the 60-minute session. Then, on the Friday, I would do less. I'd get rubbed down, I usually went to the chiropractor at the start of the week to get loosened out. After the last session before the game, I'd be totally focused, visualisation of what I was going to do on match day, plenty of sleep, eating properly, staying hydrated and keeping relaxed.

Day of the match, I'd just go totally into the zone. I wouldn't talk to many people. In the dressing room I would really get myself pumped up. If I wasn't pumped up going out on the pitch, I just wouldn't perform. Others would be calm, quiet, but I would really have to be animated. That's probably gone away from the game now. Nowadays it's very calm, level-headed. I would have been the complete opposite to get myself up to put in a good performance.

Back then anything could have happened in dressing rooms, between walls being slammed or tables being broken. I think that day is past now. Any dressing room I've been in since, from a managerial point of view, everything seemed to be calm and I think that's just that we're in a different era of the game now.

How do you rise and stay at a high level of performance?

It's about what you put in a couple of months before it. Having a good block and a heavy load of training done and being able to recognise that. Once you know you have the work done, I always went out onto the field saying, 'God help the fella I'm on today', if I knew I had the work done, I knew it was going to take a really good performance from my opponent to try and stop me.

A golden rule I had was, if I did have a bad performance, that one bad performance never became two bad performances. If you had two bad performances in a row, suddenly you're coming into a bad run of form, and a bad run of form is not good for any player.

There are some days you'll go out and the ball is just not going to run for you or your opponents are going to get the better of you. It's the psychological and mental end of it that you're not going out the next day doubting yourself. Don't be thinking what will happen if I play badly again, if I miss the first ball or there's a roar from the crowd, if you're looking to the line. You don't feed yourself with any negative energy, you feed yourself with positive energy and say what happened the last day is not going to happen again. The fella I'm on, I'm going to go out and just destroy him, I'm going to go out here and set the record straight and prove everyone wrong, that last time was only a blip and that I'm still a top player.

Paul Morris
WEXFORD HURLER 2010-PRESENT

A key part of Wexford's game-plan, Morris has shown versatility, having been used in a variety of positions and roles within the Yellowbellies' forward line. With the Model County he has won a National League title and a Leinster Championship. He has also won a Wexford Intermediate Hurling Championship with his club, Ferns St Aidan's.

Gym

It's important at a younger age to develop the right techniques for various exercises to progress; working under somebody fully qualified in this area is essential. Staying consistent with your programme for the full season is key, don't just commit to it for pre-season, keep at it and don't give up.

Nutrition/lifestyle

Educate yourself on food and eating the right combination of carbohydrates, protein and fats. Eating healthy will not only lead to you performing better but feeling better on a day-to-day basis. Keep lots of vegetables on your plate along with two litres of water every day.

Skill Practice

Any of the skills you're good at, try and perfect them. Spend time identifying your weaker areas and ask your coach for ways to improve these. If you want to improve skills, what you do outside of training is more important than what you do at training. Working on skills is one of the best parts of hurling so make sure you enjoy it. Fifteen minutes with the hurl in hand every day.

Advice to my younger self

Everything I have mentioned above, I could have been at least 50 per cent better at so if I could go back in time, I'd focus a lot more on the areas above. Looking back, one thing I'm glad of is I look back with fond memories and enjoyed it and made the best of friends. Don't beat yourself up if things don't go right for you in a match because there's another game coming. Enjoyment is the most important thing and there's lots more serious things happening in life so relax and enjoy the journey.

Mary O'Connor
CORK DUAL PLAYER 1994-2010

One of the most decorated players in the GAA, O'Connor has won seven Camogie All-Irelands, five Football All-Irelands, six All-Ireland Club titles, nine National Camogie Leagues and five Football National Leagues along with being named Camogie POTY in 2006. The four-time is all-star is the current CEO of the Federation of Irish Sport.

My love of sport was instilled in me by my family of six brothers and two sisters, a mother who loved sport with a passion and a father who balanced her passion with having a passion for farming, end of!

During my career I believed I was fortunate to be successful in sports I enjoyed playing and had a talent for, but it was only when I retired that I realised something, that yes I was fortunate to win what I did, but also that I had worked unbelievably hard to achieve everything I did! As they say hard work paired with talent can be an awesome combination.

When I retired, I didn't necessarily celebrate my career, but I did reflect deeply on how I graduated from competing with my brothers in our garden to captaining Cork to five in a row in Croke Park. While I reflected, I also remembered all the people who had an impact on me as a player, both good and bad. I hoped they knew I valued them, because they all played a part in shaping me. I reflected on different experiences: injury, loss of confidence, burnout, victory, loss, taking things for granted, being my own worst critic or how I would dwell on a problem rather than focusing on a solution! That was of course before even real life got in the way, because for a lot of my childhood, adolescent and adult life – sport was my mecca!

From that reflection, I came up with some take-aways:

Never forget the power of words, some are filled with begrudgery, some with goodwill; dwell on the words of goodwill, words of begrudgery are filled with someone else's unhappiness. I have a good saying, what the ears don't hear, or the eyes read, the heart don't feel! Also never forget the power of *your* words – use your words for good and to add value. Don't criticise! It is easy to criticise, that is why there are so many critics!

Don't play small to win big, yes have humility, but believe in your talent and don't be afraid to tell your story through actions and words. Whatever team you are a part of, family, relationships, work or sport – *be of value.*

Don't become predictable in your training or your approach, change is important, don't fight for the old, but focus all your energies on building the new. If you become predictable, you become markable or readable, then you are vulnerable to being beatable. Make mistakes; that is the only way we all learn!

Sport will not always make you happy, but when you perform, excel and win, that thirty seconds after the final whistle, after the crossing of the line, of your last play, you feel an internal explosion of delight and joy like your world is complete once victory is won! This is a feeling that drives you to keep wanting to improve and keep winning so you get to feel and experience it all over again!

Finally, people have spoken of Everest before and how everyone's Everest is different, in this world every athlete will have a different Everest, it could be a national or international medal or title! Whatever your Everest is, go after it, give yourself to the journey of trying to conquer it – the view from Everest is not crowded.

Dónal Burke
DUBLIN HURLER 2017-PRESENT

One of the best young hurlers in the country, Burke has brought the level of performance he showed at minor, where he won a Leinster Hurling Championship, through to the senior ranks. An exemplary free taker, he has won three Dublin Minor Hurling Championships and three Dublin u21 hurling Championships with his club, Na Fianna.

Gym

As younger muscles are constantly growing, it is hugely important they stay agile and flexible through exercises like stretching and foam rolling. I don't think gym exercises are hugely important until you reach your late teens. I personally never set foot in a gym until I was at minor level. I hadn't a clue how to gain muscle or become stronger. Luckily, I was able to ask for help from coaches. From my experience it is best to ask coaches for assistance when you start using the gym.

Nutrition

Just like the gym, this is an area younger athletes don't need to be worrying about until they reach minor and beyond. The most important aspects to focus on are keeping active and perfecting your skills. So for now all I would recommend on this topic is sticking to mother's cooking as often as you can.

Lifestyle

For me, I always thought it was very important to ensure I have a life outside hurling, where I can switch off when I'm not training or playing matches. I found when I would constantly play and think about hurling, I'd grow sick of it. Therefore, in relation to lifestyle, I can't emphasise enough the importance of having other hobbies as well. For me, this means I can enjoy the sport more when I am playing.

Preparation

Regarding preparation for training and matches, over the years I have realised that everyone is different. Personally, I like to relax and take my mind off hurling in the lead-up to a big game. However, I know other teammates like to completely focus in on the game in the build up to it. It's all about finding what works for you and figuring out a routine for yourself.

Skill Practice

For me the most important thing for a hurler to have is their skillset. In my opinion, first touch beats pace and power. The only way to develop your skillset is practise, practise, practise. I used to bring my hurl with me everywhere as a kid. If you're hanging out with friends or going home during lunchtime in school, always try to bang a ball off a wall for ten minutes. Every little bit you do will add up in the long run.

Advice to Younger Self

The first thing I would tell my younger self is to enjoy every minute you play as it will go by in a heartbeat. When I was fifteen or sixteen, I thought I had all the time in the world to play underage, and in the blink of an eye I'm already finished. The second thing I would tell my younger self is that help is always there for you. In relation to any of the titles above, always ask your coaches how to improve, they mightn't know everything, but they'll find you someone who does.

Conor Mortimer
MAYO FOOTBALLER 2000-2012

With his bleached blond hair, Mortimer would stand out before throw-in; after that his scores would. Mayo's second all-time leading championship scorer, the 2006 All-Star was their talisman for over a decade. He won four Connacht titles and a Sigerson Title with DCU.

To all young players out there the main things I would say regarding the start of your career are to just get out and practise, practise, practise as much as possible. Always listen to coaches. Many of them are ex-players – those guys have been there and done it.

Every spare minute you have get out kicking or doing what you are good at. This will help you improve for when you get to training or games by having extra work done. Also, the more time you can dedicate to this the better it will be for you as a player.

In today's game you need to be a twenty-four-hour athlete. Eat the correct food and drink enough water. Those who commit and have the talent will go on to become great players and not just another guy who made his county team. They will be a main player on this team and that has to be your goal.

Not to be just a county player but to be the best county player at any given time.

The main point for me is live like a footballer and just practise like you play.

Every training session needs to be at game pace in order for you to get the most out of it and yourself.

Andrew O'Shaughnessy
LIMERICK HURLER 2002-2011

A talent at underage, O'Shaughnessy won two Munster u21 Championships and two All-Ireland u21 Championships. An incredibly skilful forward, he won an All-Star in 2007, finishing as that season's top scorer. He has also won three Limerick SHC and a Munster Club Championship with Kilmallock.

You may not realise how important skill enhancement is now because the game is still just that, a game. Whether you are at training with your club or pucking around at your friend's house, you do it because you enjoy it. If you want to get to inter county level though, your skill levels will be tested to the maximum and it might be somewhat too late to develop new skills. All the more reason to engrain working, developing and practising new skills at every opportunity. If you are on your own against the gable end, let your imagination run free and have yourself playing in whatever the most important match you want is. Visualise doing something special that saved or won the match. Then practise that exact skill until it becomes second nature. Then try to develop another! Every skill is important, so skill development is continuous. Strive for perfection even though it's an illusion! Having a drive and determination towards skill development will stand you in good stead when needed the most! Little things you see on TV like a point being hit over your shoulder, an unbelievable one-handed first touch or a penalty going into the top corner all come from a twelve-year-old imagining that exact moment and practising, failing, failing, failing until it becomes practising, failing, practising, practising, practising where you then find yourself in Croke Park with the crowd wondering how could you do what you just did!

So skill development can never stop but it's not always at a training session! It is just as important and enjoyable when you are on your own or messing with your friends to keep practising and trying new skills. As a teenager, you work on skill development for yourself because you enjoy the game and take pride in yourself, your team and your family. Ultimately as you move into adulthood, take pride in the range of skills you've developed, continue to work on them and never ever forget to enjoy what you're doing, whether it's against the gable end or the Davin End!

Paul Broderick
CARLOW FOOTBALLER 2007-PRESENT

When people think about Carlow rising, one of the first names to spring to mind is generally Broderick's. The 2018 All-Star nominee has proved to be one of the sharpest shooters around. For anyone that hasn't seen it there's a great video of him on YouTube demonstrating his kicking, hitting five forty-fives in forty-five seconds.

Nutrition

Nutrition is one of the cornerstones that can help any young athlete to improve. Some people love it for its taste, some see it simply as a necessity to survive. Others may view eating as a way to socialise and connect with others.

Regardless of your view, as a young athlete it is imperative that you begin to look at your food intake through the 'my food is my fuel' lens. It's an age-old adage that if you owned a Formula 1 car, you probably wouldn't put bad quality fuel into its engine as it would not win the race. So why do we stuff our bodies with food that doesn't give us the best chance to perform to our utmost ability? There are so many choices and lots of people to tell you what's best for you to eat. And who can blame them? Everybody has a body and therefore everybody has an experience of how their body has reacted to the food they have put into it.

The quandary of what exact fuel to take on board at different stages in an athlete's career, season, tournament or game is something that will invariably change alongside your age, goal and desired body composition. However, as long as you are always open to learning more about yourself, I believe that you may one day master a balance that works for you.

I am not writing this to tell you what is best for you to eat, as that's a job for a sports nutritionist. Instead, what I would like to do is share some general nutrition principles to live by as you begin your journey as a young sportsperson.

1. Before sitting down to eat your current meal, always have your next one prepared. OK, so it's not always possible to have this done, particularly when travelling. However, you can at a very minimum decide what you are going to eat next, before you let the current meal touch your lips.

This will eliminate the chance of you snacking on something that is not going to lift that fuel gauge in the right direction.

2. If the type of food you are considering eating for your next meal was not a food fifty years ago, skip it. I always ask myself if my grandparents would eat it.

3. Create friction between the junk food and you. Anecdotally speaking, if I don't want to waste time watching excess TV, I am less likely to do so if I plug out the TV between the times I need/want to watch it. Therefore, if we ask someone to hide the food we don't want to snack on or just don't buy it at all, we are far less likely to be tempted to stray from your 'my food is my fuel' mindset. The amount of friction needed here is very small.

Lastly, I would add that young athletes should reward themselves for prolonged stints of good training or a satisfactory performance on the field of play; every now and again it is OK to wander off your nutrition path as long as you can find the way back.

Zak Moradi
LEITRIM HURLER 2010-PRESENT

Moradi made his debut on the inter-county scene when he joined the Leitrim senior team in 2010. Since then he has become a regular member of the starting fifteen. In 2016 Moradi was included on the Lory Meagher Cup Champions 15. In 2019, Moradi was a key part of the Leitrim team that won the Lory Meagher Cup.

I was born in Ramadi in 1991. Ramadi is a city in central Iraq and was home to almost half a million people at one time. Today, as a result of the Battle of Ramadi in 2015-2016, the city is destroyed and virtually empty of people.

In 2002, I moved with my family to Ireland to escape from the conflict and war in Iraq. As an eleven-year-old child, I could not speak a word of English when I moved to Carrick-on-Shannon in County Leitrim. Kurdish was the only language that I knew. In St Mary's National School, I got extra help to develop and improve my English language skills. I was determined to learn.

I was introduced to hurling by Clement Cunniffe, a well-known and respected hurler in Leitrim. Clement, a Games Promotion Officer at the time with Leitrim GAA, used to come into the school to coach children in the basic skills of hurling and Gaelic football. Taking up hurling as a sport was a major challenge for me. I never saw a hurley or a sliotar until I moved to Leitrim. In Iraq, running had been the only form of sporting activity for me. Now, hurling is my passion and this passion was instilled in me by Clement Cunniffe who gave me my first hurley and encouraged me to practise the skills of hurling as much as possible.

The skills of hurling can be broken down into skills that involve various elements of possession and select skills for specific roles or activities on a team. The skills of possession involve gaining possession, maintaining possession, releasing possession and contesting possession. The skills in gaining possession are based on stopping a ground ball, controlling a moving ball, blocking a ball overhead, catching a ball and lifting a ball. Dribbling and soloing with the ball are key components in the skill of maintaining possession. Releasing possession is done through striking the ball on the ground or overhead with the hurley or passing the ball off with one hand as a hand pass. The frontal block, flick, hook and shoulder clash are skills used to contest or tackle for possession of the ball. Select skills for specific roles on a team include: the free puck, penalty puck, puck out, shot-stopping and sideline cut. A good coach, like Clement Cunniffe, focuses on assisting players to develop the skills of hurling. However, players must have the motivation to learn and develop the skills.

I wanted to be as good as the other lads who played hurling in Carrick-on-Shannon and this encouraged me to practise the skills of the game. I had to focus and listen carefully to a coach during a coaching session to pick up the key skills of hurling. I started out by learning to hold a hurley correctly and then moved on to attempting to strike the ball. I learnt the skills through coaching and practice. Outside of coaching sessions, I just practised and practised. I brought my hurley everywhere with me and even kept it in my bedroom at night. Every day, I went to a hurling wall to practise the skills of the game. I worked on developing my skills using both sides of my body. For games, I started out playing at midfield as I had good speed and I could hook an opponent. After almost four years of dedication and commitment, I had developed the skills of hurling to a level that would allow me to dream about playing senior hurling for Leitrim.

In 2005, I moved with my family to Tallaght in Dublin. My hurling continued to improve after I joined Thomas Davis GAA club in Tallaght. I started playing with the u16 team for the club and then progressed to represent Old Bawn Community School in hurling. I continued to work on developing my skills as an underage hurler through daily practice and regular coaching sessions with the club. In 2008, I was invited to play a few trial games for the Leitrim senior hurlers. After making a good impression, I was invited to join the panel. My hurling continued to improve and I focused on developing the skillset required for a position in the forward line at club and county level. In 2012, I was selected for the Ireland u21 hurling-shinty panel for an international match against Scotland. I was part of the Leitrim team that lost the Lory Meagher Cup Final to Warwickshire in Croke Park in 2017. However, I was named on the Lory Meagher Cup Champions 15 selection for my contribution to Leitrim's run to the final. In 2019, after eleven years on the senior panel, I played a part in helping Leitrim to beat Lancashire in the Lory Meagher Cup Final. At club level, I was a member of the Thomas Davis team that won an intermediate hurling championship in 2011. As a youngster in Carrick-on-Shannon, I dreamed of playing senior hurling for Leitrim. As a member of Thomas Davis GAA Club, I dreamed of playing senior hurling for my club. The development and enhancement of hurling skills through encouragement from a role model, coaching, regular practice and self-motivation have enabled me to fulfil many of my dreams. You too can dream! Don't be afraid to follow your dreams.

Tomás Quinn
DUBLIN FOOTBALLER 2003-2012

Dublin's talisman during the noughties, Quinn's career spanned one of the biggest transformations of any team in the GAA. During his time with the Dubs he won seven Leinster titles and an All-Ireland. He was nominated for an All-Star in 2005, finishing as that championship's top scorer. Mossy is still starring for his club, St Vincent's, winning five Dublin SFC, four Leinster Club Titles and two Club All-Irelands.

Things I would like to tell my younger self

The thing that first jumps out would be to try to look at the bigger picture when it comes to being involved with a team. Sometimes things will feel like everything hinges on the next game, whether it's getting picked in the team or the outcome of the game, but while there will be important personal milestones, don't overthink things from just your personal interests. It's a team game and you should enjoy the challenge of getting into the team and making a positive impact within your squad. You are lucky to play a team sport and pushing each other to improve should be part of your daily routine, whether it is at training, matches, just playing in school or in your free time. Competing against your friends and teammates will help build a trust and understanding that will allow you to perform better as a team. Have the mindset that you want to make your teammate beside you on the pitch look better.

Everyone wants to progress individually as a player so openness to listening to coaches and trying to continually improve your skillset are starting points to developing. Fundamentals like kicking comfortably off both feet and the ability to pass with either hand can never be practised enough so these are areas that you can always work on.

Lastly, to play sports you will likely need support from your family. Parents will bring you to training and matches, they will stand on sidelines in all types of weather, they will ensure you have whatever gear is required. They get to share in the ups and downs of how these years will go. It is a great way to connect so talk to them and enjoy these days with them!

Miriam Walsh
KILKENNY CAMOGIE PLAYER 2010-PRESENT

A successful underage career saw Walsh win Leinster Championships at u14, u16 and minor grades, followed by four All-Ireland Colleges with Loreto and a Minor All Ireland. With the seniors, she has gone on to win five National Leagues, four Leinster championships and two All-Irelands. The two-time All-Star has proven to be an unselfish link-player as a vital cog in the Cats' attack. With her club, Tullaroan, she has won Kilkenny and Leinster Intermediate Championships.

Gym

I love going to the gym. My favourite thing is that I'm a member in the Watershed [Gym, Kilkenny] and I find you get more out of classes than just facing the equipment on your own. I absolutely love HIIT classes, spinning and body pump. I find these classes so useful during the wintertime especially when camogie is over. I like meeting new people at the classes, and it keeps me tipping away on fitness in the winter, which is very important too.

Nutrition

I really make sure I'm getting enough protein as it's so important when training three times a week to make sure your protein intake is good. I also find drinking water important especially the days when you're not training. I always make sure I eat protein after training or if some nights we aren't finished until late I make sure I get a protein shake or even a banana into me as it's important for recovery too.

I don't really eat any fish or red meat, so I take vitamin D supplements and iron tablets.

On a day of training, I make sure I get lots of carbs in and the days I'm not training I'll replace white bread with brown bread.

Match-Day Routine

I get up early and get moving. I listen to my music and it helps me distract myself from overthinking about the match. I always love having chats with my family and having the craic with them the morning of a match to keep my mind at ease. I try not to think too much about the game. After I get the first ball my nerves usually go away.

Advice to my Younger Self

I would go out and play every match like it's my last. The friends you make through sport are lifelong so enjoy every minute of it. Sometimes I used to take it to heart if I had a bad game so thinking back, I would tell myself to go off and stop overthinking it, go back to training and reset because not every game is going to be your best one. But most of all enjoy the moment. I used to put pressure on myself especially in club games, I would feel that everyone is depending on me, but thinking back nobody was, it was just me putting pressure on myself. Now I don't think like that. I suppose the older you get the more you realise that it's just a sport we love, so go out and enjoy the game.

Paul Geaney

KERRY FOOTBALLER 2011-PRESENT

One of the country's top forwards, when Geaney's going well, the Kingdom's going well. The two-time All-Star has proven to be one of the game's sharpest shooters, winning a Sigerson and Cork County Championship with UCC, two National Leagues, eight Munster Titles and an All-Ireland. With his club, Dingle, he has won two Kerry SFC and a Kerry Club Championship. He also represented Ireland in the 2017 International Rules Series.

Creating habits for life.

Right now you are in a great position to create new habits. What you do now will leave a lasting legacy on your future. Think of all the effort that goes into planting vegetables ... you must choose the right location with plenty of sun, ample space, good soil, irrigation and the right vegetable for the right time of year. You must plough the soil, plant the seeds, maintain the crop and then wait a substantial amount of time to reap the rewards. Even when the vegetables have grown to harvest, the job is still only half done. They must then be picked and sorted for market. The point is that the process is long with many important steps to take along the way before you can produce the goods. It is the same with producing the goods in Croke Park on All-Ireland Final day; if you didn't do the work along the way you will be found wanting. If you want to succeed in sport it takes planning, dedication, effort, time, continuous assessment, practice and a belief in yourself that it will all be worth it in the end.

The three areas I suggest you focus on are:

1) Skill Practice

2) Nutrition

3) Lifestyle

Briefly to explain why I chose these three is because you will never have the amount of time available to you as you do right now. Ever.

1) Your skillset can be worked on every day. The best way to improve is through visualisation, role play and deliberate practice. What I mean by deliberate practice is that when you are shooting at goal, you do so at game pace. Pretend there is a defender trying to dispossess you or block you down. You should do this with every skill you practise. There is strong evidence to suggest that the best time to acquire skills is between four and twelve years of age. Therefore, you should maximise this window and learn as many as possible while you can!

2) Nutrition is a key aspect for athletes' training and performance. If you can create good eating habits, eat whole and nutritious foods, avoid processed and sugary foods then this will be a great start. Top tip: learn how to cook. It's fun and a great way to know exactly what you are putting in your body.

3) A healthy lifestyle will give you many benefits, mentally and physically. A routine is good, but make sure to have fun and break it once in a while too. Athletes require eight to ten hours' sleep, so factor that in. Practise time-management, keep tabs on your screen time and do at least twenty minutes of vigorous exercise every day is a great start!

*Remember, skills need to be practised or they will be lost. You need to 'pick the weeds' (self-assessment) and get rid of bad habits regularly. Some crops are annual and results can be seen in the short term but others take years to develop like an apple tree so don't lose focus! This does not guarantee a good crop, but it is the building blocks to give you every chance to succeed.

Conor Cooney
GALWAY HURLER 2012-PRESENT

An All-Ireland winner at both minor and u21 levels, Cooney showed a lot of promise at underage. He has since lived up to that promise winning a National League, three Leinster titles, an All-Ireland and All-Star. With his club, St Thomas', he's won five Galway titles (three as captain) and one All-Ireland club title.

Gym

Gym work and conditioning has become more and more important since I've started playing inter-county. It's important to develop strength and power but I think it's most important as a means of injury prevention. We do a lot of prehab and activation work which can be tedious but is very important.

Nutrition

I always find eating healthily is a habit. If you make small changes and are consistent with them they can make a big difference.

Daily routine

Getting to bed early and leaving down your phone is the best piece of advice I could give. I find reading a book helps me to wind down whereas if I'm on my phone I find it much harder to sleep. Turning on a blue light filter on the phone just isn't as effective as leaving it down altogether.

Match-day routine

I try to have all my preparation done before match day. I'd have my gear ready from the day before. I'd be sure to be well hydrated and have gotten plenty of sleep in the days leading up to the game. Then I get up early and have a good carbohydrate-rich breakfast. I go outside and puck around. Eat a light lunch about three hours before throw in. I'd try to get out on the pitch before the game and decide whether to wear studs or moulds.

Skill Practice

When I was younger I tended to practise what I was already good at instead of identifying a weakness and working on that. You can always improve so I always look at what I can do different or better. If another player is good at a particular skill I watch them doing it and try to learn from that. Then I try to apply it in my own training.

Advice to younger self

Enjoy every game you play.

Michael Quinlivan
TIPPERARY FOOTBALLER 2012-PRESENT

A star at minor level, winning an All-Ireland minor title in 2011 against a Dublin team with many future All-Stars, it's safe to say Quinlivan has lived up to the hype and gone on to be one of the deadliest forwards in the modern game. A Munster Championship winner, he has achieved success with his club, winning three Tipperary titles and a Munster title with Clonmel Commercials. Quinlivan also picked up an All-Star award in 2016.

Advice to my younger self

I think that one of the main messages I would tell a younger version of myself would be to keep believing in myself. There are plenty of people out there who will try to knock your confidence and tell you that you are not good enough. Don't mind them, listen to people you trust and don't give up. When I was in secondary school, I didn't start on any Gaelic football team from second year until I was in sixth year. I had people who told me I wasn't good enough, but I eventually made my breakthrough. At fifteen and sixteen years old it seemed like the be-all and end-all, but looking back it actually just made me stronger, and helped me to keep believing in myself no matter what.

John Conlon
CLARE HURLER 2009-PRESENT

At u21 level Conlon won a Munster and All-Ireland championship with the Banner. It is easy to see he has been a leader with any team he's been involved with, winning a Fitzgibbon with NUIG, two National Leagues, an All-Ireland and an All-Star. The Clare Captain has also achieved success with his club Clonlara, winning Clare and Munster Intermediate titles and a Clare senior title.

As an athlete and a hurler, you must be able to tick as many boxes as possible when it comes to preparing your body to be in the best shape it possibly can be. This consists of proper nutrition and sleep to fuel and revitalise your body sufficiently, working hard in the gym to avoid injuries and make you stronger on the field of play and developing your skills of hurling not only at training, but on the nights you have to yourself where you go to the local GAA field to get extra shooting or striking in.

If I was to give advice to my nineteen-year-old self, starting to play inter-county, it would be to prepare accordingly, ask as many questions as possible of coaches, and always evaluate yourself and see what aspects you can get better at. I am a very positive person and try not to dwell on negatives in general. I try to approach hurling in the same way. After a match or a training session, I will try to focus on the things I did well and the areas I need to improve. I am probably known for my power and strength rather than speed. Speed is an area that I have really tried to improve on throughout my career. I have done this by asking coaches for advice, watching YouTube videos and researching information in this area. As a result, I have improved my acceleration and deceleration. Looking back to games in my late teens/early twenties, I am certainly leaner now and have improved my speed work. This did not happen overnight; it required a lot of hard work and is an area I must continue to develop and improve.

I am very interested in nutrition and have researched lots of information with regard to this. When I first began my inter-county career, knowledge and understanding of food wasn't as prevalent. Now most county teams and even club teams see the value of having a nutritionist on board.

'The more you put in, the greater the reward.'

Kieran Donaghy
KERRY FOOTBALLER 2004-2018

'Star' first came to the Kingdom's attention when playing against them with the Underdogs. He made his debut the following season at midfield. His move to full-forward transformed a Kerry team supposedly in crisis into All-Ireland champions. The 2006 Footballer of the Year enjoyed a highly successful career, winning two National Leagues, eight Munster Championships, four All-Irelands, three All-Stars and represented Ireland in three International Rules Series. He has also won a Kerry SFC and a Munster club championship with Austin Stacks. The Sky Sports pundit is also a classy basketball player having won two Super League titles and two Super League cups with the Tralee Tigers. He is currently coaching with the Armagh footballers.

How did basketball influence how you played football?

There are a few things: peripheral vision, quick hands, good hand-eye coordination. One of the big things would be decision making and game management.

In basketball there's so many decisions going through your head, that when it comes to football you get used to making the right decisions for your team. Of course, there are extremely smart footballers that will make the same decisions that would have never played basketball. But if you look at any of the players that have: Jason Sherlock, Liam McHale, me, Ronan McGarrity, Mike Quirke. Whenever we were playing for our teams, it would be rare any of us would make a bad decision, the execution might be bad, but the decision making would normally be good. I think this was a huge factor that helped me throughout my career.

In the 2014 All-Ireland final, I scored 1-2, I touched the ball eleven times and I made ten correct decisions. This meant I had eleven key decisions to make. In a basketball game I could have two hundred decisions a game.

What's the best advice you were given during your career?

It was when I wasn't enjoying football. When Aidan O'Connor took over the Junior C team in Austin Stacks, he asked me into the squad. I said, 'No, I'm playing basketball with the Irish u17s at the moment, I'm not enjoying football.' He said he'd make sure I enjoyed it and that they always had the craic at training. 'Come up, if you're having fun keep playing, if you come up and you don't have fun, don't play.' There's no point in doing something if you're not having fun. Of course, there'll be tough times when you lose, but in general you must enjoy what you're doing.

How do you stay motivated in a game if the ball isn't coming up to you?

Full forward is a very tricky position in the modern game, I think you have to have serious levels of patience. You have to have the courage to stay inside, especially in my position and role as a 'big-target-man', that would be a huge part of being successful in that role. There would have been some games where I possibly wouldn't have seen the ball for fifteen minutes, you start looking over at the bench wondering 'Are they going to take me off?' You might think to run out the pitch and get on a soft ball, but that's not your job for the team. Your job for the team is to stick it out. Whether you're a full-forward or a corner-back, whatever the job you're given, that's the one you have to do.

As an inside forward in the modern era, it is getting tougher to find space. Dublin have really utilised the backboard cuts and a lot more teams have started doing it now to get free that way. You regularly see Con O'Callaghan make a move towards the sideline before doubling back into the space he's freed up for himself, creating 1v1 situations.

It is harder now to win ball in closer to goal, the days of Bomber Liston and Mikey Sheehy are done now. I always slag them about how it would be great to play in the time you were man-to-man, where you just had to win it and once you beat that man you were away. Nowadays there's swarm defending, group defending, zonal marking.

It's a tough position now on any team, especially if you're living off scraps or not getting much ball. But you just have to stick it out and you have to be patient and aware of your job for the team. If your job is to stay in close to goal and try and get scores, then that's what you have to do.

How did you practise catching high ball?

I would never say that I ever put too much effort into it. I did the whole throwing the ball off the wall, kicking the ball off the wall. There's an old video of Mick O'Connell doing it, outside his house in Valentia. Try to meet the ball at its highest point, kick the ball off the wall with a run and time the jump so you're reaching it at its highest point. It's an important part of the game and it's a huge skill in the game. I think the great components of the high catch are fondly remembered in the history of the game.

Did you have any superstitions or rituals before games?

I sat on the seat second from the back on the bus, on the right always. There was a fire escape there, so it had extra legroom. Once I got my perch there early on in my career that's where I sat for the next thirteen or fourteen years. Gooch used to sit opposite me, and I would never get off the bus ahead of him. We used to always be the last two to get off the bus for big games. I got a sense of confidence walking in behind Colm in the different cauldrons and atmospheres around Ireland. I used to say to myself, 'This fellas' on my team, if he's on my team we must have half a chance.' We'd give each other a nod and he'd go ahead of me, so I was usually the last one off the bus.

I used to have a *piseog* about wearing the socks up. It was something I always did as part of my uniform. As part of the old-school Kerry footballers, their uniform was socks up. There was a great footballer in the Stacks, the late John Melvin. When Stacks won the County championship in 1994, he gave me his socks after that game. A pair of smelly, sweaty, deep-heat laden Stacks socks. I wore them for three or four years after that, I had one of them on under my sock in my first game in Croke Park as a Kerry minor.

Also I used to wear the skins, bicycle shorts. I always felt more comfortable in them. Were they *piseogs*? Maybe. They wouldn't have been common when I started wearing them. It would have been looked at as a bit off maybe, but nowadays everyone's wearing them, it keeps your hamstrings warm and helps with recovery.

Don't be a bully

Nowadays I think bullying online is far more prevalent than in person. Don't send that message, don't put that message up in the group that you know will drag two other people in your class down. I was bullied when I was younger and it's just a horrible thing to do. You'll regret it so much when you're older if you are a part of it.

Be big enough to say if others are doing it to leave it off. If somebody's not going to be your friend, because you stuck up for someone being bullied or you've called somebody out for doing nasty things, then they weren't really a friend to begin with. When I was back in school there were all these kids, they all thought they were cool, but really when it came down to it, the bullies and the cool guys, not many of them went on to do anything.

Welcome constructive criticism

You should be able to take constructive criticism in the same manner that you take praise. You have to be able to take constructive criticism from coaches, if you're ever going to make it in life or as a player. If you take it, learn from it and bring it on to your next thing. You'll have a much better situation whether it's in sport or general life.

Eoghan O'Gara
DUBLIN FOOTBALLER 2008-2019

A handful for any defender, the Templeogue target man will be remembered as not just a great forward, but a great goal scorer, particularly important goals. A key part of Dublin's five in a row success, O'Gara finished his career with a medal haul of a Sigerson with DCU, five National Leagues, ten Leinster titles and seven All-Ireland titles.

Preparation

This word covers everything for me in terms of getting ready to deliver a performance and gives me the confidence that I have done everything within my power to be ready for a training match or a competitive fixture.

It covers a large number of areas both mental and physical that are hugely important to being ready to give the best version of yourself when it's needed most.

As I got older my preparation changed and was modified. Some things I did a lot of like gym, strength work and extra fitness conditioning work were replaced with more rest and recovery like stretching, yoga and swimming. My only focus was to get my body and mind in as good a place as possible so that I could perform well and get into the team or stay in the team.

Another hugely important part of this preparation was my mindset and my confidence. I realised as the years went on just how important these areas were and always looked for ways of improving them and figuring out what worked best for me. I tried to stick to routines with the things that helped me in this area such as positive self-talk (affirmations), guided meditation and certain playlists of music at certain times before performance.

John Heslin
WESTMEATH FOOTBALLER 2011-PRESENT

A Sigerson winner with UCD, Heslin has been Westmeath's talisman for the past decade. His performance in the 2011 International Rules Series granted him a brief spell with the Richmond Tigers in the AFL. He has also won five Westmeath SFC with his club, St Loman's.

The most important part of forward play is scoring! In the modern game it can often be neglected, but having that eye for goal and continuously practising the execution of score-taking is vital. In order to work in an attacking unit you must also be unselfish in your movement. Moving into positions to make yourself available to receive the ball will automatically create space for your teammates to get into possible scoring positions.

Another main feature of modern forward play is defensive play. The full forward line is often the first line of defence, and hard work from the forward unit aids defenders and general defensive play, ensuring that the team is as best set as possible not to concede.

As a forward in the modern game it is important to have an array of skills. Of course scoring ability is a must; to be an attacking asset to your team you must be able to move around a number of positions and able to adapt to a particular game scenario. The basic skills such as catch, kick, tackle and hand pass must be executed to the highest standard and practised repeatedly regardless of the level you're playing at.

Aidan Fogarty
KILKENNY HURLER 2003-2014

Taggy first played for the Cats at minor level winning a Leinster championship. He later won a championship at intermediate level, winning a Leinster title. A call up to Kilkenny's u21s soon followed where he won u21 Leinster and All-Ireland championships. The 2006 final MOTM won seven National Leagues, ten Leinster Championships and eight All-Irelands as a key part of that great team. He has also won a Kilkenny JHC with his club, Emeralds.

How do you play to your best even when thousands are watching you?

It comes through experience. I'm playing hurling since I was seven years of age. As I got older and went through the ranks, crowds were always building before I got to Croke Park. Most people try to phase the crowd out and try to concentrate on themselves. It can be very daunting, but when you're playing hurling for so long, you start to just concentrate on the game. The crowds are there but they're at the back of your mind, more than anything else.

Were you talented as a child in sport?

I guess I was. I was always sport orientated. I remember sports day in Url-ingford, where you'd have 100m sprints, 1500m, different kinds of lengths, long-distance running, short-distance running. I used to win a lot. I think one day I won all the races. I remember coming home with a pile of medals. I was very sporty, very active, I played basketball and soccer. Most sports I turned my hand to, I would have picked up fairly quickly. Hurling in Kilkenny was always going to be the number one sport and that was the one I concentrated on.

What do you eat before a game?

The day before, you're trying to carb up really. I would have eaten:

8:30-9am A bowl of porridge with fruit, cup of tea.

11:30am I'd try to eat every two and a half to three hours. To avoid letting your body be hungry, just replenishing your system all the time. I'd have a scone and a cup of coffee.

1-2pm Time for carbs! A pasta dish with chicken.

4pm a snack. Nuts or some kind of protein with a bit of fruit.

6-7pm I'd have a steak dinner. Steak, potatoes, veg. Nothing major, not too much oil or butter.

Before bed I'd have a bowl of cornflakes, because you won't be waking for eight hours. That's eight hours without eating.

The day of the game, it's all planned out by the management. I'd get up and have my bowl of porridge with a bit of fruit. Then we're on the bus to Croke Park. We'd get a couple of sweets, fruit pastilles and a Lucozade just to keep the sugar levels high. Sandwiches and soup in the hotel at about 1:30, with a match at 3:30, that's it for the day. Then after the match everything goes!

What's the best piece of advice you got during your career?

Control the controllables. I didn't get that advice until I was probably about twenty-five or so. I was hurling for Kilkenny, beginning to get bogged down on things, not playing well. I was concentrating on things that were out of my control. Control the controllables! That meant look after myself, get myself in the best possible shape I could, be in the best possible position to get picked, look after my diet and so on. These are all things I can control. Getting picked, I can't control that, so there's no point in worrying about it. Control the controllables.

Advice to Young Players

Live your life as much off the field as on the field. I gave 120 per cent to hurling, no doubt about it. I probably neglected some things off the field in my own life. Like I wouldn't have gone to functions because I was training the next day, or even if I had a match the next week, I wouldn't have gone, so I wouldn't have to talk about the match. These are things I regret now. If you're happy off the field, you'll be happy on the field and it's reflected in your hurling.

The best piece of advice I would give to someone is live your life in every aspect, on and off the field. Experience new things, travel if you want, go to functions. Everything in moderation though. There's times and places where you can't go, you can't be going to something every Saturday or Sunday night because you have to look after yourself too. Family parties, things like that, whenever you can go, go! Don't be worried about talking about hurling or people getting into your head, or you think you mightn't play well because you might go to a function. Go to that function and live your life as much off the field as you do on it. Give life 100 per cent and give hurling 100 per cent.

Neil Flynn
KILDARE FOOTBALLER 2016-PRESENT

A star at underage level winning a Leinster Minor Championship and strong performances at u21, Flynn was called into the Lilywhites' senior team. A proven free taker, he has shown to be a key part of the Kildare forward line.

Skill Practice

It's hugely important for an inter-county footballer to have two feet, especially as a forward. It makes you twice as hard to mark, leaving your defender guessing as to which side you're going to go. It all comes down to practice and the hard work you put in to improve your weaker foot, at training but more importantly away from it.

As a free taker, practice must become part of the weekly routine, whether it's getting down early or staying late at training or getting out kicking on your night off. To make your practice really beneficial my advice would be to keep track of your shots scored/shots missed in a kicking session and look to improve every session.

Ciara McAnespie
MONAGHAN FOOTBALLER 2007-PRESENT

Coming from a family steeped in Monaghan GAA, one could say it was in McAnespie's genes to star for the Farney County. The three-time All-Star has proven to be one of the deadliest forwards around. A National League winner she has also won an All-Ireland Intermediate Club Championship with Emyvale.

Gaelic football has played a major part in my life from a very young age, having started with my club at u8 and progressing to county level from u14 to senior at present. Looking back, I have learnt a lot along the way and the game has evolved so much over the years to become one of the fastest growing ladies' sports.

If I was to give advice to younger players out there now who want to be the best they can be, there are a number of areas I would recommend them to focus on. Firstly, they need to focus on themselves to prepare themselves physically and mentally. Every player has their own unique physique. In my own case I was very small, but that didn't hamper me on the pitch. When I started county football, the gym was introduced into our training regime. At first my perception of the gym was that of bodybuilders, but as I soon learned, that doesn't have to be the case. The gym didn't mean that I bulked up. What it did was help improve my joint strength thus improving my balance and posture and also my running form and power. This really helped compensate for my physical size as it allowed me to work on areas that benefitted my game. Push ups, planks, crunches along with weights helped me build on my strength and I also found the change of scenery in the gym helpful.

Nutrition was another area that was so important for me. As I moved up to county level, I was training a lot more, so it became very important to fuel my body and to eat sufficient food to give me that extra energy I needed. I know there are many pressures on young girls in particular to watch their weight and this can lead to under eating, but if you want to compete at the highest level in ladies' football, it is vital you eat properly. Good nutrition contributes to a healthy and strong body, which will help improve your football as it will help improve your strength, training, performance and recovery.

Another area that young footballers need to focus on is their lifestyle. This is another area that a good balance is important. You don't want football to be seen as a chore. You want to be able to enjoy it, so it is important that you get the balance right. Go out with your friends and enjoy your free time as much as possible. A final bit of advice to any young player would be that there is always room for improvement. Go out on your own and practise your shooting. Don't just presume you'll learn it all at training. Those extra few minutes that you put in yourself could make the difference during a game. And finally enjoy what you're doing. It is very important that you enjoy playing the game. If you are enjoying it, you will perform better. If you push yourself too hard and that enjoyment starts to waver, then you must re-evaluate what you are doing. Enjoyment is the most important thing because if you enjoy what you are doing, you'll want to keep at it.

Brian Carroll

OFFALY HURLER 2002-2016

A successful underage career saw Carroll win an All-Ireland colleges title with St Kieran's and a Leinster Minor title. A key part of the Faithful's attack, he won two National Leagues, four Railway Cups and was twice nominated for All-Stars. With his club, Coolderry, he's won five Offaly SHC and one Leinster Club Championship. He retired as Offaly's second highest all-time championship scorer and now hosts 'A Hurler's Life' podcast.

Gym

I try to hit the gym twice a week for a full body workout concentrating on staying lean. I don't lift too heavy and I'm not chasing a six-pack. I aim for about 30-40 minutes max working hard and enjoying it while I'm working out. I often dread going, but I feel great after doing it.

Nutrition

It's important to eat as healthy as possible by choosing fresh meat, veg and fruit. Treats are no harm – we all love a treat! – but in moderation. Don't be obsessed with your diet, but be conscious of making good decisions. Please, please avoid 'sports' or 'energy' drinks!

Match-Day Routine

I like to practise frees the evening before a game just to get my eye in, then have a good carb-heavy dinner and plenty of water. On the day of a game, I have a good breakfast of porridge and berries and pasta and chicken about two or three hours before throw-in. I like to watch about twenty minutes of a game of hurling on TV and then I have a few pucks off the wall just before I leave, bless the hurls with holy water, say the Hurlers' Prayer and off I go!

Skill Practice

You honestly can't practise enough on your own, particularly in your teens. Challenge yourself and try to improve every aspect of your game. Don't always be in your comfort zone. But most importantly get the basics right before you try the fancy stuff!

Advice to Younger Self

Don't take the game or yourself too seriously. Enjoy it more, smile and you'll get more from the game. Remember why we play and love the game of hurling!

Dean Rock
DUBLIN FOOTBALLER 2013-PRESENT

One of the game's top forwards, Rock enjoyed success at u21 level, winning two Leinster Championships and an All-Ireland championship. Probably the best free-taker in the country, the three-time All-Star has been a key part of the Boys in Blue's recent successes. A Sigerson winner with DCU, he has recently become Dublin's all-time top scorer, a feat unlikely to be beaten as he is still only thirty. He has won five National Leagues, eight Leinster titles and seven All-Irelands. He has also achieved success with his club, Ballymun Kickhams, winning two Dublin SFC and a Leinster Club Championship.

FREE TAKING
How do I practise frees?

Practice has evolved for me over time. Initially I would have gone kicking quite a lot – hundreds of balls a session – but soon realised it was taking its toll on me and I was tired come games. Now instead I take thirty to forty kicks a session, but with real purpose and intent, trying to put myself into game scenarios in my head.

When did I start a routine and has it ever changed?

I would have always had a style of kicking off the ground or from my hands and I've added tweaks to my routine down through the years as my knowledge of shoulder position, proline (a point in the distance I want the ball to travel towards) and commitment to the strike has evolved. I'm always learning whether it be from my own practice or from my coaching.

How do I replicate pressure kicks?

We play a lot of games in training which allows me to practise my free kicks in competitive situations. When I'm not practising, I can prepare via visualisation and imagery.

Advice to young players

Listen to your coaches. Ask for feedback from a coach/person you admire/ trust. Ask for honest evaluation of your game and then from the identified areas for you to improve you should tailor your training towards improving these, whether it be skills, fitness, speed, strength etc.

Graeme Mulcahy
LIMERICK HURLER 2009-PRESENT

Following Fitzgibbon success with UCC, Mulcahy was called into the Treaty County's senior ranks. Since then he has proven to be one of the game's top forwards, winning an u21 Munster Championship, three NHLs, four Munster Championships, an All-Ireland and an All-Star. Mulcahy has also won three Limerick Club Championships and a Munster Club Championship with Kilmallock.

I have three main areas of advice for players looking to develop.

Firstly, there are many things that make someone a good player, it can be speed, strength, quickness of the mind, agility. Some of these will come naturally to players and some will not. We may possess several of these strengths, but no one player has it all! One thing however we all have in common is the ability to work hard, and the ability to self-assess. I would advise young players to take the time to recognise your own personal strengths and weaknesses and set out to work on improving these. If I was twelve again, I would work harder on my striking off my right side. It has been a weakness in my game since I was young and one that I never took the time to address until recent years.

Secondly, I advise young players not to pigeon-hole themselves into one sport or one hobby. As a child I enjoyed a lot of sports: soccer, football, rugby, tennis. I was also very interested in other things like chess, card games and anything that challenged my brain. I think the fact that I was encouraged to try all these different things made me a better all-round hurling player. For instance, I would say my footwork is a strength of mine that was mostly developed from playing soccer. Take Kieran Donaghy as a good example. You can easily see how the skills he developed on the basketball court were of huge benefit to him on the football field and vice versa. There are learnings and skills that you will get by exploring your interests that will be transferrable to the game you end up playing or job/career you end up pursuing, so I would encourage you to try everything and never dismiss or discourage someone from trying something different!

Lastly, there are a lot of fad diets, fad gym programmes and other mis-leading information out there today readily available to young kids who want to pursue sport at a high level. I would advise you not to believe every documentary you watch, article you read, advertisement you see. Much of the content you see online, on social media or streaming sites is produced solely to sell you a product or a certain lifestyle that in reality will not help you reach your goal and may even hold you back. Trust your managers, teachers, coaches and parents. Believe me, they know best.

Conclusion

That's the end of the book! I hope you enjoyed reading it as much I did putting it all together.

When I started putting this book together and contacted Self Help Africa and the first couple of players, I only had two goals in mind: to give the next generation of GAA players a resource that wasn't there for generations past and to raise a bit of money for charity. I like to think that I have succeeded in both.

To finish I would like to share with you three pieces of advice I would like to tell myself if I was twelve again.

Identify weaknesses in your game and work on improving them. At u12 I would bounce the ball as soon as I got it which led to me being regularly dispossessed. At u14 high fielding was a weakness; most of my Féile photos are me going up for a high ball and it landing somewhere behind me! At u16, the outside of the boot addiction. When it comes off I still think it's the most attractive way to kick a football. If you have trouble picking out a weakness, ask your coach. They'll be pleased to see you're interested in improving and will be more than happy to help.

Practise on your weaker side. As many of the players said throughout you'll be tougher to mark and will have more options when it comes to decision making as you'll be able to use both sides of your body. Ideally you should be able to kick the ball six different ways: instep, laces and outstep off either foot.

Develop a strong first touch. If the last year and a half of adult football has taught me anything it's that if you don't win the ball first time, it's unlikely you'll get a second chance at it.

I hope you can adopt some of the learnings and habits throughout the book to help you in your future. Thanks for reading and best wishes!

Mol an óige agus tiocfaidh sí,
Seán O'Sullivan

Acknowledgements

Hopefully this won't be the last book I write, but at risk that it is, I feel there are a few people that it's important to thank.

First and foremost, I would like to thank all the players for taking the time and energy to contribute; this book obviously would not have been possible without them. With a project this size I feel it is important to have the right people involved and that is what I like to think I've done here. I know it's a cliché, but they truly are fantastic ambassadors not just for their counties, but for our games and country as a whole.

Mick Bohan for the fantastic foreword. I met Mick on a brilliant workshop he ran in my club pre-Covid. He completely disproves the saying 'nice guys finish last', as obviously he is a serial winner, but also one of the nicest and most genuine people I've met within the GAA.

Marty Morrissey for his lovely foreword; I think it sums up his love and passion for our national games. For me, Marty has been the standout voice of the GAA during my lifetime, the warmth and approachability he displays on the television is the same as how he comes across in real life.

Those at the O'Brien Press: Helen Carr, my editor, Emma Byrne, Design Manager, for the great cover design and layout, and Prin Okonkwo for her help with picture research.

Ciara Tallon and Alan Kerins of Self Help Africa for getting involved and trusting me with what was only an idea at the time.

Brian Carroll, Shane Stapleton of OurGame.ie and my own clubmen, Niall Cooper and Tom Ryan, for putting me in contact with some of the players that I otherwise would have struggled to get in touch with. It would be difficult to find a member of Na Fianna that hasn't benefited from Niall's presence within the club in one way or another, be it through training sessions, camps, coach education or as a role model on the field of play.

All the managers and coaches I've had to date for keeping me interested and involved in both Na Fianna and the GAA, especially Ricky O'Sullivan and Kieran Brennan.

My current manager and coaches, Tiarnán Ó Dubhlainn, Pat Brennan and John Lynch, for the countless hours given to me and my teammates between meetings, training and matches.

My teammates for welcoming me into the J8 family and for the guidance and support they've given me in my first two years of adult football.

Finally, my parents, Ricky and Róisín, for always ensuring I got to training and matches or that I at least had a lift, also my mam for proofreading the book before I submitted it to The O'Brien Press. And my sister, Siobhán. Firstly, for her continued confidence in me and secondly to her and her fellow front-liners at Beaumont Hospital.

Picture Credits

Front cover

The players' tunnel (photo: Brendan Moran/Sportsfile).

Back cover

Croke Park pitch (photo: Ray McManus/Sportsfile).

Goalkeepers: clockwise from top left:

Gary Connaughton (photo: Ray McManus/Sportsfile), Aoife Murray (photo: Diarmuid Greene/Sportsfile), Brendan Cummins (photo: Matt Browne/Sportsfile), Ciara Trant (photo: Piaras Ó Mídheach/Sportsfile), Niall Morgan (photo: Brendan Moran/Sportsfile), Eoin Murphy (photo: Harry Murphy/Sportsfile).

Full backs: clockwise from top left:

Keith Higgins (photo: Brendan Moran/Sportsfile), Eoghan O'Donnell (photo: Ray McManus/Sportsfile), Cathal Barrett (photo: Stephen McCarthy/Sportsfile), Bríd Stack (photo: Brendan Moran/Sportsfile), Pamela Mackey (photo: Matt Browne/Sportsfile), Aidan O'Mahoney (photo: Brendan Moran/Sportsfile).

Half backs: clockwise from top left:

Ken McGrath (photo: Brendan Moran/Sportsfile), Kevin Cassidy (photo: Brian Lawless/Sportsfile), Elaine O'Meara (photo: Stephen McCarthy/Sportsfile), Tiernan McCann (photo: Ray McManus/Sportsfile), Aaron Kernan (photo: Sportsfile), Tommy Walsh (photo: Brian Lawless/Sportsfile).

Midfielders: clockwise from top left:

Rena Buckley (photo: Brendan Moran/Sportsfile), Noel McGrath (photo: Sam Barnes/Sportsfile), Derek Lyng (photo: Brendan Moran/Sportsfile), Sarah Rowe (photo: Sam Barnes/Sportsfile), Gary Brennan (photo: Diarmuid Greene/Sportsfile), Colm Galvin (photo: Brendan Moran/Sportsfile).

Half forwards: clockwise from top left:

Denise Gaule (photo: Matt Browne/Sportsfile), Podge Collins (photo: Brendan Moran/Sportsfile), Declan O'Sullivan (photo: Brendan Moran/Sportsfile), Lyndsey Davey (photo: Piaras Ó Mídheach/Sportsfile), Neil McManus (photo: David Fitzgerald/Sportsfile), Mattie Donnelly (photo: Brendan Moran/Sportsfile).

Full forwards: clockwise from top left:

Ciara McAnespie (photo: Sportsfile), Kieran Donaghy (photo: Ramsey Cardy/Sportsfile), John Mullane (photo: Stephen McCarthy/Sportsfile), Ross Munnelly (photo: Matt Browne/Sportsfile), Conor Cooney (photo: David Maher/Sportsfile), Miriam Walsh (photo: Piaras Ó Mídheach/Sportsfile).